The Most Jewish Thing I Could Do

Coming to Christ from the Old Testament side of the cross

MATT SCHECHNER

Copyright © 2019 Matt Schechner.

All rights reserved. No part of this book may be reproduced, stored, or transmitted by any means—whether auditory, graphic, mechanical, or electronic—without written permission of the author, except in the case of brief excerpts used in critical articles and reviews. Unauthorized reproduction of any part of this work is illegal and is punishable by law.

ISBN: 978-0-5782-1222-7 (sc)
ISBN: 978-1-4834-9698-6 (e)

Because of the dynamic nature of the Internet, any web addresses or links contained in this book may have changed since publication and may no longer be valid. The views expressed in this work are solely those of the author and do not necessarily reflect the views of the publisher, and the publisher hereby disclaims any responsibility for them.

Any people depicted in stock imagery provided by Getty Images are models, and such images are being used for illustrative purposes only.
Certain stock imagery © Getty Images.

Scripture quotations taken from the New American Standard Bible® (NASB), Copyright © 1960, 1962, 1963, 1968, 1971, 1972, 1973, 1975, 1977, 1995 by The Lockman Foundation
Used by permission. www.Lockman.org

Lulu Publishing Services rev. date: 02/04/2019

Contents

1. Growing Up Jewish in NY. 1
2. What Did Your Parents Think?. 9
3. The Shema. 27
4. The Tabernacle and the Holiness of God 31
5. It's The Most Christian Thing I Could Do 49
6. The Messiah-ship of Jesus. 61
7. My Burden For My People. 97
8. Our Witness to the Jewish People. 111
9. The Resurrection and the Messiah 133

1

Growing Up Jewish in NY

I was raised Jewish and grew up in Great Neck, New York, just minutes from Manhattan, "the city" as it is called. Exit 33 was our exit off the Long Island Expressway. I remember it all like it was yesterday. Thinking about that I realize that at my age I don't want to really want to focus on how long "just yesterday" really was. Let's just leave it as "some time ago," that feels like yesterday.

So we lived just outside the city, and it was nice because you could just drive right in, in no time. This is of course assuming that it was not rush hour, because then you could just sit, and it would be being anyone's guess as to how long it would take you. I have no idea what it would be like today, but I can imagine. But it was a great place to grow up, and lots of good memories come up thinking about those days. I have lived out west for almost thirty years now and may not even recognize it if I went back. It's funny though because I remember talking with people when I did live there about what it used to be like years before when they were younger, and they would tell how different it was, and then I would try to piece together landmarks and the open spaces they would describe that were now covered with office buildings and homes. I remember when I watched the original *Sabrina* movie with Audrey Hepburn, Humphrey Bogart, and William Holden. It was filmed on Long Island close to where I grew up and when I realized where it was set I found myself concentrating more on the scenery than the story line. I couldn't believe how much it all had changed. It was beautiful when I lived there but then it was gorgeous, pastoral and open. I could see how it was when people had described it to me, where before I could only guess. In one scene Audrey Hepburn is at the Glen Cove train station and William Holden comes driving up in his little sports car to give her a ride. It was all so open and tree-lined, completely unrecognizable to that of today. What a scenic and idyllic place Long Island was and still is I'm sure to a large degree.

I loved the neighborhood where I grew up, it's old windy roads, roads that were originally designed hundreds of years ago to take you and your horse-drawn carriage through the woods to your destination. The streets are still tree-lined and the neighborhood still shows signs of its past. The street names give an idea of what it was like with names like West Woods road, our street, and Meadow Woods road, Schoolhouse and Horseshoe lanes. It was great living there because you had peace and quiet and all the beauty that it offered, and again, Manhattan right at your fingertips.

This was also a good place to be if you were Jewish because our way of life thrived there and there was much acceptance. I didn't have any idea how much of an anomaly this whole situation was, we were so accustomed to, seeming so normal to me to be Jewish and have most people around me be Jewish. As well, many other ethnic groups also lived there and everyone lived harmoniously together. It wasn't until I moved west that I realized how much it wasn't always the norm.

The famous New York food was another perk of living there. As kids we would always be trying to scrape up enough money to go and get a slice of pizza at Sebastian's place, Center Pizza, who had seen us almost every day since we were old enough to walk there. They were like part of our extended family. Another favorite hangout was the local Israeli restaurant where we would have falafel and talk for hours with all the people who congregated there. For something to do we would head into town and then before we knew it the day would be over, it was getting dark and we were late for dinner and had to rush home. The food was outrageous. One time, and this is almost embarrassing to repeat, upon graduating high school, a friend of mine had a going away party at his house and I knew where they bought the potato salad from. I asked them if they got this at the Great Neck Deli. His mother turned away from her conversation and asked, "How in the world did you know that?"

Living in a predominantly Jewish community also provided for some uniquely Jewish scenarios. Again, you don't know how unique until you move away. The one that most comes to mind was a Thanksgiving when I was around nine years old. It had snowed the night before, and by midmorning the roads had been plowed and were pretty clear except for the usual remnants of the previous night's storm, snow still piled high all along the side of the streets. The season and all the snow added to the usual holiday morning calm and beauty. Most people had already begun preparing the Thanksgiving dinner. Everyone was inside avoiding the cold and preparing for their special day with their families.

My neighbor across the street was planning to have a very large group over for dinner and they were preparing an enormous amount of food. They had put the turkey on the trunk of their car in his garage to keep it fresh and cool, and out of the way before cooking it. I'm sure that they also needed to make room in the kitchen because of the size of the thing. They left the huge bird on the car, staying fresh in the cold, waiting for the oven, with the garage door open.

All was very quiet in our house except for the usual sounds coming from the kitchen as my mother was already busy cooking away. In one flash of an instant it all changed. I heard my mother shout; slap her hands down hard on the kitchen counter, then just run out of the house. She just flew. She never ran like that. She never ran. We had no idea what had gotten into her.

We all hurried over and crammed together around the dining room window to see what was happening. Then to our amazement we saw our mother running across the lawn, trying to catch my neighbor running down the street, her arms flailing frantically as she went, another woman right behind her, both in hot pursuit of our German Shepherd, who was in the lead with the giant turkey in her mouth. She was galloping triumphantly, now trying to pick up speed as they were getting closer. The dog turned suddenly and headed across our lawn, probably thinking that if she could just make it home, she would be safe and could enjoy her prize. Her error in judgment gave my mother the chance to head her off and get the turkey back.

Completely out of breath my mom gave the turkey back to them thinking the whole thing was rather humorous. They didn't. The woman's husband said emphatically that he didn't want the turkey any more. With his hand held up in front of him, expressionless, he told us how he wouldn't even consider it.

Not for reasons you might think.

You're probably assuming it had something to do with their evening meal meeting the ground a couple of times or being grossed out by the dogs grip on it? That wasn't it. My neighbor said he didn't want the turkey any more because since it had been in the dog's mouth it wasn't kosher anymore.

We all still laugh at that one when we tell it and act it out over and over, even after all these years. Distinctly Jewish was certainly the description for life in our town. By the way, we did eat that turkey for dinner that night. It will always go down in our history as the meal our dog caught for us. She did of course get her share. What else could we do, she earned it.

As I grew up in our little town, in customary fashion I was sent to Hebrew School as soon as I was old enough, as almost all of the kids I knew were. The first school they actually sent me to was a Jewish preschool, I kid you not. We had it all. The preschool was at the local Samuel Field YMCA in Queens. I remember playing with dreidels and doing puzzles. I grew up thinking that everyone had dreidels. (For those of you who don't know, it is a little toy, a spinning top given to Jewish children during the festival of Hanukkah. We all played with them at school).

When I was older my parents continued to send me to Hebrew School. This time it was held at our Synagogue in the heart of our town. We went every Tuesday and Thursday as soon as public school was over, until 5:30. We also met on Saturday morning from eight o'clock until twelve noon. The study was comprehensive, learning to read and write Hebrew, with a study of Jewish history and culture, as well as celebration of all of the high holy days and festivals.

One day they held a school-wide contest with a guaranteed prize for the winner. I don't remember what I did, or how I did it, I just remember that I won. I can't even remember what the questions were, but I'll never forget the prize. One day when we were all assembled in the auditorium they used the opportunity to announce the winner. I was called up on the stage. They asked me what I wanted for a prize. They told me to pick any topic for the subject of the prize. They said to choose whatever interested me, so I didn't hesitate with my answer. I said sports. As soon as I said it though, I thought, "Oh no! Why did I say that?" But he repeated back to me and I felt it was too late to change my answer. I was stuck. The reason I felt so bad was because I knew they would relate it somehow to a lesson in Judaism, and now I thought that I had made it almost impossible for them to do that. I didn't realize that soon enough so I lamented to myself, "Where is this poor man going to find anything about Jewish people and sports?" There were many, many great Jewish men that I certainly looked up to, but not many famous Jewish athletes that I could remember. Whitey Ford of the Yankees did live a few blocks away, but I doubt he was Jewish. I was so mad at myself for putting them in that predicament. I kicked myself mentally all day over my answer.

Well time went by and I had forgotten about the contest. Then they announced that they were ready to give out the prize. They called me up to the office to pick it up. I wondered what they got me as I walked to the office. I started to feel guilty all over again. When I got there the head of the school was smiling and handed me a wrapped gift. It was heavy. I tore the paper off and it was a book. "Wow," I thought, "This is great." I felt so relieved. "I don't know how, but they did it." I was so happy. And I still have to admit, surprised.

The book was called, *The Jew in American Sports*. "Man!" I thought, "And it is so thick!" I figured a book with that title would be a pamphlet, or worse yet a three-fold brochure. I opened it right up and began curiously flipping through it, as I had to know what was in it. Of course, I have to admit, half the book was about Sandy Kofax.

By the way, when I tell that joke to groups when I am speaking, I get an interesting, mixed reaction. People over fifty laugh right away. The ones who are younger look at me like, "What?" "Who?" and go blank. "What is he talking about?" they say. They don't get it. It's funny to see that reaction.

For those of you who don't know who he was, he was one of the best pitchers in major league baseball ever, and played for the L.A. Dodgers in the sixties, and was Jewish. The book also had a lot of boxers in it. That surprised me as well. They looked as though they should be accountants working for Arthur Anderson, but with tough expressions on their faces and some rough edges. I learned that there *were* a lot of Jewish boxers around at one time, but mostly a long time ago. This is certainly not a phenomenon anymore. I personally never knew anyone from my predominantly Jewish hometown who grew up and became a boxer. Doctors, yes. Boxers, no. I noticed though when watching the movie *Rocky* while working on this book, that the character of the trainer/manager in the movie for Rocky, Mickey, was Jewish. Mickey Goldsmith was his full name, and was portrayed to have been a professional boxer himself, with his heyday in the 1920's.

One of the many things that benefited me greatly growing up where I did, and is also a strong part of my culture, (which I respectfully admit is also part of many others as well), was the strong work ethic. It was a given that you would achieve, that you would succeed at whatever you decided to go into. You were taught to cultivate your mind fully and not waste it. There was a definite spirit of achievement. There was an accompanying optimism, a confidence, a surety of accomplishment that was passed on. Hard work to achieve that end was not shied away from either, this was also expected. My grandfather told me that anything worth achieving I would have work hard for. He proudly taught me as we walked through the streets of New York City as he told me his whole story of how he grew up there and that it was tough, but he made it, he worked hard and persevered, and I could too, and never to forget that. He took me to the building in New York where he first started working and then to where he began his business in the beautiful and distinctively New York, the Chrysler Building. I think this was also characteristic of generations from the past cross culturally more so than today. I don't see this spirit in the present day in as many circles as it once was. Thinking back on the high school I attended, the average final grade average in my high school class (we were given a score for our grade totals based out of a 100 % and not a 4.00 scale), was 85%. To not finish High School was almost unthinkable, and this was cross-cultural as well. It didn't matter, it was strongly looked down upon by even the kids, and was almost unheard of in my immediate neighborhood.

I had a professor in college that I was friends with who talked of this same thing. He also was Jewish, growing up in Brooklyn. We hit it off almost immediately, both being Jewish and having similar experiences, and also being so far from it all drew us close together quickly. He said he experienced the same phenomena, the same environment growing up. We talked about how different the expectations are in most other places in the country and especially now. He talked about the crowd he graduated with in high school in Brooklyn. He said that his gaining a PhD. didn't get him much attention, it was expected. He said, in his full New York accent and accompanying bluster, "Hey, what I did," he paused, looking around, "My doing this," "I was like the loser." He sat back in his chair and shook his head. "Yeah, it was nothing compared to what everybody else did." He was being facetious of course, but was saying that where he lived the people really took education seriously along with an attitude of doing the best you could in everything, and they did.

There were other positive benefits I took away from growing up Jewish in New York, the education, the arts, going to all the museums since I was young, being exposed to so many cultures. It seemed everything was happening right there. I remember a humorous cover from *The New Yorker* Magazine that summed up the whole New York attitude about this. It showed a map of the Unites Sates with New York in great detail, prominent, on one end, which summed up the East coast, and then there was nothing but empty land, barren ground, all the way to the Pacific Ocean. That became a popular framed picture that I remember seeing hanging up in more than one person's house or apartment. Our city seemed like the center of everything.

I am grateful to God for many things, a nice place to live, all of our needs graciously met, a loving family, good friends, and I also am very grateful that I grew up Jewish. I love being Jewish, I love my people. I love the history of my people. I am thankful most of all to God for my salvation, and that my eternal destiny now and forever will be with Him. But I am also so glad that I was brought to the Lord as a Jew, from the Old Testament side of the cross. This is what this book is about, and most importantly how natural and fitting it is as a Jew to recognize and love the Messiah who has come for us, who without I would not be honoring the one true God, the Lord Jesus Christ.

It is amazing to think of what God did through the Jewish people: for example, the promises that were made and that could never be broken and never were. They had the privilege of communion with him and through them the Messiah of the world would come, and has come. We have to understand the story that lead up to His coming to redeem mankind, to make sense of all this, a wonderful story of the Jewish people to which He first came. A total understanding of our lives as Christians cannot be understood without grasping who the Jews were. And in discussing this belief in the Messiah who did come, it inevitably leads us to the next question which just as assuredly follows, that I hear all the time.

2

What Did Your Parents Think?

When people ask me to tell my story the first question is usually, "What in the world did your parents think?" This almost inevitably comes up first when I discuss my faith in Christ and my background as a Jew, and especially for some reason my adding being from New York. I don't know what it is about the N.Y. part along with being Jewish, but that seems to really get them going. "You're Jewish, you're from New York, grew up there, and you're a Christian?" They ask. It's funny also because the response is different out west than it is when I tell people in New York. When I tell people out west, they'll usually respond with something like, "Oooh, how interesting," even if they are a little perplexed. But in New York you tell someone and you'll probably hear, "You're a Jew and a Christian," and then in typical New York fashion, "What's the matter with you?"

Their reaction makes more sense when you take into consideration the many mis-characterizations and falsehoods that abound about what Christianity is and where it comes from, and about Judaism for that matter. But a close study of both shows that barrier is not really there at all. The root, the very basis, of Christianity is found in Judaism. Also seeing how there are Jewish people who reject the Messiah and are sometimes quite vehement about it, can make people wonder how it is possible that I am a Christian. To the watching world there seems to be so much animosity between the two. To many people the two faiths are antithetical, they are polar opposites.

Another factor that drives a wedge between the two and forms peoples' perceptions of the incompatibility of the two is the way Jews feel hated by Christians, because Jews have been persecuted in the past by some claiming the name of Christ. This is something no Christians should ever, under any circumstance, contribute to. Any person who claims to be a Christian and is involved in such behavior will certainly have to answer for it before God. Jesus said they will know us by our love. That is what should characterize us. Any Christian reading this should be extremely upset about anyone who persecutes another, the Jewish people included, and we should be more determined than ever to go out into the world and show the love of Christ because that is what is supposed to be in our hearts. Romans chapter 11 of the New Testament (Romans 1:1-36 NASB), deals with this subject, dashing any possible sentiment on the part of any Christian of anti-Semitism, or of any feelings of superiority toward the Jewish people. But the opposite attitude has helped foster the sentiment that many Jewish people have seen Christianity as anti-Jewish. And although some people in the past, claiming to be Christians, have engendered this sentiment, it is the furthest thing from what Christ taught and stands for.

So I can see where they get this notion and seem surprised, and how they find the whole thing to be a bit of a shock, but the point of this book is to show that it shouldn't be. According to all that Judaism encompasses, all that it teaches, it is so fitting, so natural to be where I am in terms of what I believe, recognizing Jesus as the Messiah. The evidence is overwhelming. I accept this solely by the grace of God, but once He opened my eyes I could see how fitting it was. As a result of this mercy my eternal destiny is changed.

So they ask me about my belief. Then the next inevitable question comes up, and usually with a gasp almost as though they totally forgot about that part, "What about your parents, oh my goodness, what did they say?" I tell them about how I did of course tell my parents, and the answer was that they were not real happy. My parents are so different and as expected so were their reactions. My dad's reaction was more severe, my mother wanting to just avoid it. She was not happy, but didn't want to think about it. Just wanted to forget it happened. My father, as I said, was another story. They have been divorced for many years so of course I had to approach each of them separately.

My dad is an active member of his Jewish synagogue that he attends. He has no compulsions about talking about his faith for which I was glad, but my father's views saddened me, as I am sure it does God, because he thinks he is serving God when he is rejecting Him. Isaiah, the great a prophet of God, speaking for God to the people, recorded in the Old Testament, spoke of a God who in His great love reached out to a people who would not have Him, holding out His hands to them all the day long, to a rebellious people who would not come (Isaiah 65:2).

We talked; we walked through the Old Testament, the whole story of redemption, the great promise of the Messiah who would come through the Jews, bringing redemption, one which the Jewish people longed for. I talked of all of the evidence in the Old Testament, The predictive prophecies from Jewish prophets which unmistakably describe Him. We saw the great and grand detailed descriptions of this coming Messiah predicted 700 years before His arrival. He listened as I talked of this, putting it together as concisely as I could, and said nothing, standing and listening in his usual stoic manner, with me typically being unsure of his reaction. Then after an awkwardly long pause he just said

"Anytime someone claimed to be from God, *we*, (meaning the Israelites), killed them."

"Oh," I thought, "This is going to be fun."

Sadness filled my heart as I recalled the words of Jesus Himself.

> *"Jerusalem, Jerusalem, who kills the prophets and stones those who are sent to her! How often I wanted to gather your children as a hen gathers her chicks under her wings, and you were unwilling"* (Matthew 23:37).

Just as with the words of God recorded by Isaiah, God is saddened by rejection of the salvation He offers. He is completely sovereign, and everything that He decrees to pass will indeed happen (Isaiah 46:10), but takes no delight in the punishment of the unrepentant (Ezekiel 18:33; 33:11). It is crushing to see one of God's people reject His anointed Messiah. It is so joyous when someone accepts Him and is a cause for great celebration and elation. This again shows what is expected as predicted by the Scriptures and how natural and fitting belief in Jesus as

Messiah is. It was predicted that the Messiah would be rejected by His own people and we see that when we look at Isaiah 53 (as we will in depth later in this book, Isaiah 53:1-12). The Hebrew prophets came to the people from God to correct them in their disobedience to Him, their turning away from His ways, and were rejected and killed. Jeremiah, a prophet of the Old Testament, complained bitterly to God about how these people (his fellow Jews), mocked him and persecuted him and wanted to kill him (Jeremiah 12:1). He was God's spokesman to the people, speaking God's words. He prefaced what he said with *"Thus saith the Lord,"* because he came from God Himself. The people did not want to hear it. This is recorded in the Hebrew Scriptures, what is called by Christians the Old Testament. This is what Jesus was talking about when teaching about the treatment of the prophets sent from God. He lamented over how the people rejected these men of God as they did Him. This as I said was predicted in the Old Testament and was no surprise to Jesus. But as we saw in the previous verses, God's great love and compassion has never wavered, and still longs for His chosen people to come to Him.

I could not believe the reaction of my father and how it fit what the Scriptures foretold. My heart was broken by his reaction, as nothing is harder than a family member who does not see the truth. My heart breaks for anyone, Jew or Gentile (non Jew) who rejects this message, who does not see the truth of the Messiah who has come. My father did not see how God is offering the great blessing of salvation and he would not, as Jesus said, because he was unwilling. I never stop praying for him and maybe some day God will take out that heart of stone toward the Lord and put in a heart of flesh as the prophet Ezekiel prophesied so many years ago (Ezekiel 36:22-28) to those who would believe, as He did with myself and countless others. He did not want to hear what I had to tell him. Sadly, the parable of the Marriage feast from Matthew 22 also came to mind. It just makes you want to weep as our Lord did over Jerusalem. I can only imagine how our Lord felt as he spoke his lament over Jerusalem. Even my love and mourning over my own father could not even be compared to the love of God for His people. In Matthew chapter 22:1-14, Jesus tells the parable of the Wedding Feast, an analogy of God's invitation to the marriage feast of the Lamb (Jesus) in heaven. The Messiah did indeed come for His people, the Jews first. Upon their rejection He went out to the Gentile or non-Jews. This gospel, or good news of salvation, now goes out to the world.

> "The kingdom of heaven may be compared to a king who gave a feast for his son. And he sent out his slaves to call those who had been invited to the wedding feast, and they were unwilling to come. Again he sent out other slaves saying, "Tell those who have been invited, "Behold, I have prepared my dinner; my oxen and my fattened livestock are all butchered and everything is ready; come to the wedding feast. But they paid no attention and went their way, one to his own farm, another to his business, and the rest seized his slaves and mistreated them and killed them."

This enraged the king in the parable and it did bring judgment. He sent his servants out to bring in others who were not originally invited and brought them in. These others guests that the king sent out for were to represent the Gentiles, or the non-Jews. The original invited guests were the Jews. These are the ones that Jesus came first for. It is as John recorded in his gospel in chapter 1, verses 11-12:

> "He came to His own, and those who were His own did not receive Him. But as many as received Him, to them He gave the right to become children of God, even to those who believe in His name."

As we have said, the prophets of the Hebrew Scriptures, the Old Testament, told of this rejection of the predicted Messiah, by His own people (Isaiah 53:1,3; Psalm 118:22). This was what was told hundreds of years before the Messiah's actual arrival. This Messiah was the one to whom every faithful Jew watched and waited for, longing for the day of His coming.

But also back in the Old Testament the prophets told of a remnant (Isa. 6:9-13; 1:9; 10:20; 10:22; Jer. 4:27; Zech. 13:9; Hos 1:10-11), true Israel (Romans 9:6), the ones who would believe, who would not reject Him, and were faithful to God, they would always be there. This is true in the New Testament as well. This remnant was the many Jews who recognized Jesus as the promised Messiah. The early Christian church was almost exclusively made up of Jews. Then it spread out from there and to the Gentiles, as many as would receive Him. Which is just how Jesus described it would happen, coming first for His people and then having the ministry move out from there; from Jerusalem, to Judea, Samaria, and to the outermost parts of the earth (Acts 1:8).

This makes me think of a time recently when I was talking with a fellow Jew and we had a wonderful time enjoying each others company. We became close friends and spent a lot of time together and with other friends. It's so hard especially with close friends, because you certainly don't want them to spend eternity separated from God. I just wanted to cry out, "He has come! He came for us! The promises of God have come!" I did tell him but had to tone it down of course. But it is hard, because the truth is so glaring and so much more wonderful! All of these verses in the New Testament show forth the love God has for His people and for their eternal destinies. They bring out this longing for my brothers and sisters, my fellow Jews, to see the truth and be reconciled to God, the great loving Father. I long for them to realize the great patience and love that God shows bringing in His people to Himself. He is holy and we are not. We have only rebelled against His cosmic authority and do not deserve the mercy He extends it to us anyway. People still reject it. I don't know how they can complain about this. They certainly don't want justice, because relying on that means we would be judged on our goodness to which none of us could stand. King David, writing under the inspiration of the Holy Spirit, prayed before God in Psalm 130:1-4,

> *"Out of the depths I have cried to You, O Lord. Lord, hear my voice! Let Your ears be attentive to the voice of my supplications. If You, O Lord, should mark iniquities, O Lord, who could stand? But there is forgiveness with You, that You may be feared."*

David knew how he compared to God and how he could never measure up to the perfect standard (that we had when He created us, but our sin destroyed, Romans 5:12) that is needed to be in heaven with Him and

His holiness. He pleaded with God for mercy because that was all that could save Him. He knew if God judged him based on his sin he would certainly fall, as we all would. As a result we should have the utmost gratitude to God as well as an appropriate awe and reverence for Him.

The apostle Peter, a Jewish man, expressed this sentiment of God's great love and patience in waiting for all of His people to come to repentance. Peter spoke of how God is patient and seems slow to some but is not, He wants to allow people time to repent.

> *"The Lord is not slow about His promise, as some count slowness, but is patient toward you, not wishing for any to perish but for all to come to repentance"* (2 Peter 3:9).

And the apostle Paul, another Jewish man (who God used to write most of the New Testament), taught of this as well, saying how we should not take lightly the kindness, tolerance and patience of the Lord which leads us to repentance (Romans 2:4).

Another story that Jesus told came to mind in my discussion with my father, the Parable of the Vineyard Owner (Matthew 21:33-46). This parable of Jesus also tells the story that I was trying to relate to my father, the story of God's redemption, which began with His people. The nation of Israel was frequently referred to as "the vineyard" in the Old Testament. And as is evident from the reaction of the Jewish leaders to Jesus' telling of stories such as this one, it is also very evident they understood the connection. But this parable gives a capsule summary of the events in the story of redemption, beginning in the Old Testament and continuing in the New Testament. It tells of the story of the formation of the nation of Israel and the sending of the prophets of God to speak to the people for God, their rejection, the coming of the Messiah, and His rejection and death. Jesus told the people:

> *"Listen to another parable. There was a landowner who planted a vineyard and put a wall around it and dug a wine press in it, and built a tower and rented it out to vine-growers and went on a journey. When the harvest time approached, he sent his slaves to the vine-growers to*

> *receive his produce. The vine-growers took his slaves and beat one, and killed another, and stoned a third. Again he sent another group of slaves larger than the first; and they did the same thing to them. But afterward he sent his son to them, saying, 'They will respect my son.' But when the vine-growers saw the son, they said among themselves, 'This is the heir; come, let us kill him and seize his inheritance.' They took him, and threw him out of the vineyard and killed him. Therefore when the owner of the vineyard comes, what will he do to those vine-growers? They said to him, He will bring those wretches to a wretched end, and will rent out the vineyard to other vine-growers who will pay him the proceeds at the proper seasons." Jesus said to them, "Did you ever read in the Scriptures, 'THE STONE WHICH THE BUILDERS REJECTED, THIS BECAME THE CHIEF CORNER stone; THIS CAME ABOUT FROM THE LORD, AND IT IS MARVELOUS IN OUR EYES.' "Therefore, I say to you, the kingdom of God will be taken away from you and given to a people, producing the fruit of it. And he who falls on this stone will be broken to pieces; but on whomever it falls, it will scatter him like dust."*
>
> *When the chief priests and Pharisees heard His parables, they understood that He was speaking about them. When they sought to seize Him, they feared the people, because they considered Him to be a prophet."*

It is important to note that this rejection of Jesus is not unique to some of the Jewish people as in the above story Jesus told. Romans 5:10 and other places in the New Testament describe how we are all opposed to God and enemies of His before His Spirit changes our hearts to be inclined to Him, to love Him.

> *"For if while we were enemies we were reconciled to God by the death of His Son, much more, now that we are reconciled, shall we be saved by His life."* (Romans 5:10)

My own reaction was certainly not positive when someone presented this whole story to me before I believed.

When talking with my father I also thought of the one who was to precede the coming of the Messiah. This was John the Baptist. The herald of the Messiah, the one who would announce the arrival of the Messiah as was predicted in the Old Testament, right at the end of the book, the last prophecy. It was from the prophet Malachi, that many would listen as indeed they did, and as Malachi prophesied,

> *"Behold, I will send you Elijah the prophet before the great and awesome day of the Lord comes. And he will restore the hearts of the fathers to their children and the hearts of the children to their fathers, so that I will not come and smite the land with a curse."* (Malachi 4:5-6)

Many Jewish people came out to see John and repented, turning from their ways, turning to God, and anticipated the coming Messiah. He powerfully witnessed to all of them, crying out as the prophet Isaiah foretold of this coming event:

> *"The voice of one crying out in the wilderness: prepare the way of the Lord; make straight in the desert a highway for our God. Every valley shall be exalted and every mountain and hill brought low; the crooked places shall be made straight and the rough places made smooth; the glory of the Lord shall be revealed, and all flesh shall see it together; for the mouth of the Lord has spoken."* (Isaiah 40:3-5)

John the Baptist came to make the way for the King, Jesus, the Messiah. He stood in the desert and preached. Many, many Jewish people came to see him. It was a startling time for the Jews because they had not heard a voice of prophecy for over four hundred years, since Malachi (the time from the last book of the Old Testament, ending the Jewish Scriptures and the events of the New Testament).

He had such a big impact that the Jewish leaders from Jerusalem sent representatives to question John. They asked him if he was indeed the Messiah (the Christ) or the one who would come before him as we talked of from Malachi (John 1:19-27). It was clear to them that he was sent from God because of the way he spoke and from his impact on the people. John answered that he was not the Messiah but that they should prepare for His arrival soon, this being the coming of Jesus.

As I had mentioned earlier, my mother's beliefs were quite different from my father's, and so consequently would be her reaction. They had always been polar opposites all throughout all my life so this was not surprising. My mother's reaction much more closely represented the majority view in the community of ethnic Jews today. That majority view is that one that is not as concerned regarding aspects of the Old Testament as I was presenting them. My mother was not very orthodox in terms of her faith, but was adamantly opposed to my following Jesus. This I have found to be true in almost every witnessing situation I have ever been in with a Jewish person; that most ethnic Jewish people do not believe in the truth of the Hebrew Scriptures, in the sense of them coming from God Himself, and are not practicing Jews in that sense as the ancient Jews were.

My mom didn't say much at first and hasn't really said a whole lot since. She will come out with something every now and then. She is much less outspoken than my father, and has totally different views on being Jewish. She did say once that she thought I was out of my mind, but since I had heard that so many times growing up, that could have been the reason why it didn't have much effect on me now.

All kidding aside, in my youth I'm sure I earned that remark, but now I certainly didn't. That is because my faith is placed in one who is altogether perfect, and altogether holy. Following someone like that would certainly be a very sane thing to do, unless you take a view different from the one about Jesus as presented in the Bible. If you take the view of many that Jesus was not the Messiah, was not divine, but that He was still a good moral teacher, and one of many spiritual guides available, this presents a problem. Jesus clearly claimed divinity. If Jesus claimed these things and was not who He claimed to be, He would have been out of His mind, because He claimed to be God. Do that today and see where that lands you. If He wasn't crazy then He was a liar, but again

He can't be and also be a great prophet or great moral teacher. Liars are not great moral leaders. The other alternative is He was who He said He was and this demands our allegiance. (This is the Lord, Liar, Lunatic trilemma developed by C.S. Lewis). So my mother would certainly be right in saying that to me if indeed Jesus is not who He claimed to be, but I believe that He proved who He was many times over, the most conclusive being His resurrection from the dead. (We cover this thoroughly in Chapter 9 on the Resurrection of Jesus).

Besides being the most Jewish thing a person could do as the title of this books suggests, it is also the most appropriate thing they could do. I want to honor God as God and the first commandment says that we should have no other gods *before Him, coram Deo*, before the face of God. Certainly this is of paramount importance to God, as it has to be. God is a God of truth, and abhors all falsehood which is the trademark of the one who is called the father of lies, namely the devil. And if we love God we love what He loves and follow what flows from His essence. This includes truth, love, mercy, justice.

The evidence is abundant, and is shown to be the truth in accordance with God's Word. The Old Testament prefigures the Messiah in its rituals and symbols of the life of the Israelite people, a people whose lives surrounded a pattern of preparation for the arrival of the Messiah. All of the sacrifices the Jewish nation offered to God prefigured the one great sacrifice to come, that of the Messiah, offered for all of His people. This was the culmination of millennia of build up and preparation for this moment. This is story of the Old Testament. That's the thing about Christianity, it's all about Him and its all because of Him, as the Old Testament was.

I also know when I am criticized simply about following Christ that I am not really the object of the criticism. It is directed at the one they have issue with, this is God. As a kid I remember when I would be at odds with my parents, I would wonder if I done something to actually commit the offense to my family and deserved their disapproval and correction. I remember mulling it over. "Did I really do something wrong to offend them, was it really that bad?" Sometimes it was obvious to me and sometimes it wasn't, and many times I didn't realize it at all until much later as an adult, upon having my own children. But I would turn it around and around in my head and try to figure it all out, and see if I had caused the offense against them. I was doing that now with presenting to my mother what I now believed about the Messiah, Jesus. This time with my mom I knew that I hadn't. Our Lord and the message of salvation He presented, is described as a "rock of offense" (1 Peter 2:8), a stumbling block for the Jewish people, and foolishness to the Gentiles. Here again is the predicted reaction. But certainly this message never deserves correction or ridicule, although it will certainly provoke it due to the character of man since the fall in the Garden, since sin entered the world.

We subsequently have to expect some trouble from presenting this "rock of offense." Jesus said that we would have tribulation, this coming from the fact that we proclaim Him and His gospel. He told us that we would have that in the world, but to take courage because He has overcome the world. Suffering in the name of Jesus, being persecuted for your faith in Christ brings blessing. And this of course does not include creating the offense, being offensive, contentious, and then claiming that you are being persecuted. And although it was hurtful and was difficult to deal with my family and their reaction, it pales tremendously in comparison to what my brothers and sisters face now and have suffered in the past for their faith. And I am much more concerned with my family's eternal destiny than anything that would happen to me.

> Jesus said, *"Blessed are you when men say all manner of evil against you <u>for My sake</u>"* (Matthew 5:11)

I wasn't thinking about this at the time but it is comforting to know that it will certainly happen and that you are not unique, and this will happen to all who follow Christ and faithfully stand for Him. But he sees and rewards those who stand in the midst of rejection. Jesus quoted the Psalms of the Old Testament in John 15:25 which also predicted rejection of the Messiah by many,

> *"But the word that is written in their Law must be fulfilled: 'They hated me without a cause."* (Psalm 35:19 or 69:4).

So rejection by many of the Messiah and His message was predicted in the Old Testament, and in the New Testament.

There are also of course many who believe that it was all according to God's plan for salvation, the gathering people from every tongue tribe and nation whom He purchased with His own blood (Revelation 5:9). For a new believer who may be reading this, it may explain the reaction you are getting from people when you present the truth you have recently learned.

After I first told my mother about my following Christ as the Messiah I really wanted to understand, to get at the root of what it was about my faith that bothered her. I wanted to be able to share this good news with her. The Messiah that all Jews had longed for had come. This message that Jesus gave warning of a time when the whole world will come into account for their lives and will fall short of God's standard, one which they had at the beginning but was lost through man's sin, needs to be dealt with. And only by counting on the righteousness of Jesus which is a gift of God through faith can we ever as sinful people stand in the presence of a holy God. To a person hearing this who is without the Holy Spirit enabling them to see it, this will be foolishness (1 Corinthians 1:18). Natural man, fallen human beings (which everyone is as a result of the fall of Adam, the result of his sin, see Romans 5;12), cannot understand without the Holy Spirit making them spiritually alive (1 Corinthians 2:14; John 3:3; 2 Corinthians 5:17). These people will put their faith/trust in Jesus who perfectly meets that standard for them.

But I wanted to know what my mother was thinking, wanted to properly hear her out, to know where we should go in our discussion together. We have to first understand each other and I wanted her to know that her thoughts mattered to me. I also wanted her to know that was a part of my respect for her. It was so important to me for her to know that I wasn't disagreeing with her just to be right, or to simply rebel against her authority or teaching. This is the truth and as such I desire for her to see this as well. For if it is true everyone does. If Jesus is right and I believe He certainly is, everyone needs to hear this message. We all have to respond to truth in a similar fashion in our lives. Sometime the consequences are more urgent than others. After a natural disaster we see the temporary change in people and the natural and urgent focus on these matters. But then after time has passed this world consumes them again and they go back to their old habits of living.

This was brought up in a conversation I had with someone recently and I was told by that same person some time later that they don't believe in what I presented. And I asked him to examine it all to see if it was true, and the importance of following what has been shown to be true. He said he's not worried about it and wasn't that interested. I mentioned to him that there was too much at stake to feel that way. It is fascinating how people will take so much interest and time with so many things in their lives in comparison to their eternal destiny.

I wondered initially if my mother's objection had much to do with God. I also wondered if her protest stemmed from the fact that she thought I was worshipping the wrong God, or that I was violating the Old Testament with my beliefs, as that would be very important for me to know. If it was something else I would want to know as well so I could answer her on the basis of the objection. This was all done ultimately out of love for her. If what I told her is true it matters greatly. If I truly believe what Jesus clearly taught us, that without Christ and trusting in His goodness, she would surely be lost for all eternity; if we truly believe those words, and if we truly love people, we would do all we could to have them know the truth about Christ and the salvation He alone offers to all who believe. This is why He told us to go out and tell people about it, and to go to all nations (Matthew 28:19-20).

But I had a feeling that she was not going to tell me that I was not worshipping God the way that I should. That frankly would have been an easier objection to deal with because what is presented in the Hebrew Scriptures would give testimony to what I was telling her, it would lead to this conclusion.

The concern should always be that of God before we consider any of our personal interests. But I didn't suspect that her concern was over God and the proper worship of Him.

While talking on the phone with her the occasion came up to ask her what it was about my becoming a Christian that bothered her? I gently asked her what it was about my belief that she was upset about. It became apparent pretty quickly that she didn't really want to talk about it. She sort of "hemmed and hawed," as we used to say, around the issue and was not answering me. That kind of went on for a while and I didn't really get anywhere. I was trying to still find out what exactly the problem was and I hoped she could hear my genuine concern for her. Her objection to it was important and I wanted her to know that it was not my intention to upset her unnecessarily. I knew that if it wasn't so important I would not have kept pressing the issue. She then said, "Your sister is raising Kate (my niece) Jewish. We finally were getting closer. I then asked her why she thought my sister was raising Kate Jewish? She answered because we're Jewish. And then I gently raised the point that no one in our family even practices the High Holy Days (including the biggest Jewish holidays Rosh Hashanah, Yom Kippur, and Passover) really, and no one in our family ever goes to Temple anymore, and that I really didn't understand her concern in light of their practice of Judaism. I remember being so thankful to God when I was talking to her because this was all coming out so gently as it should and with compassion. I truly was putting this forth as softly and respectfully as possible.

She told me again that my sister just did that, and it was because she was Jewish, ignoring the comments I had just made a few minutes earlier. I asked her again why it is important to do that if she doesn't observe the holidays, why do it if she doesn't follow the beliefs? I even asked her if it would make her happier if I did the same thing even though I didn't really think it was true, and she said yes! I was stunned by what I was hearing. My belief could have been totally superficial and not honoring to God whatsoever, and that would be acceptable as long as I did not profess belief in Christ. Why hold to a belief if you don't really think it is true? But I have encountered that many times with my fellow Jews. Also in essence it would have been acceptable to denounce the truth of it, the objective reality of the Jewish faith, but still say that I am Jewish by faith and that my kids are also. If I never went to Synagogue again that would not have mattered either. How could this not matter in the case of what religious belief you hold? I practice it only if I believe it is true, not merely to carry on a tradition.

I offer here a side note. This is very symptomatic of the culture we live in today, where ultimate objective truth is being pushed aside, and people can live in the cognitive tension of it and the contradiction it upholds. How it is fine to raise your child as a Jew but adhere to New Age religious thinking as my sister does. You can send your kid to the Jewish synagogue and not think it's true. The reaction would probably be something like, "Well, as long as it's true for you." It is considered acceptable as long "as it works for you" as some might say, or if it makes you feel good. These types of things cannot be determinates for truth. If something is true it exists whether we believe it or not. If the God of the Bible exists, He is there whether we believe in Him or not. And an equally important point is that if indeed He does not exist, all my belief in Him cannot conjure Him up.

This is not only a fact in the case of our religious faith it is also true for day to day living. We could not survive one day without making decisions that show our belief in that truth and our actions display this belief. Even the decision to wait for a green light reflects our knowledge of an objective reality that we know to be true.

So this went on for a bit, where we were discussing my sister raising her daughter Jewish essentially because we were raised that way. The conversation turned to discussing how God equates to all this, because again that is the real issue. I asked her where God factors into all this. Shouldn't who He is and our love for Him be the reason for worship, not any other external or personal reasons? She didn't answer that question unfortunately.

There was a short pause and then she said, "Your sister did it for me."

I felt sad because God should be the main focus of all of our lives. There are some Jewish people, (and Christian people for that matter), who go to services because of tradition, or go through the motions of their faith to please their parents. I know people who have taken up a certain faith to please their spouse. None of these are good reasons. We should only practice our faith if we believe that it is true. Especially in terms of what the Bible claims about eternity, the question to ask yourself is how is this belief going to help me at all if the Bible is right about its claims?

I was recently in a conversation with a Jewish man who told me that he goes to Temple for social reasons. He said he likes the ceremony and the traditions but does not believe that what the Old Testament teaches is true. I am sure that there are many Jewish people who believe in the reality of their faith, but I do feel that there are more people who are Jewish by religious faith and do not believe that what the Old Testament says is real and true. This is also in the Christian faith as well, with professing Christians denying the essentials that make up that very faith they supposedly hold to.

This is also seen in Christian seminaries, institutions whose role it is to train the future Christian leaders. Most take the view that the Bible is not God speaking to us, and that it does contain error and if you believe in the reality of all that the Bible says you are incorrect, out of touch with modern critical scholarship, and considered old fashioned and outmoded. Jesus certainly believed and taught that the Bible contained accurate historical truth, Mosaic authorship of the Pentateuch (the first books of the Bible), as well that it was indeed God speaking to us (Matthew 11:23-24; John 8:56; Matthew 4:4; Matthew 22:31).

I mentioned to this man I spoke of above, that the Bible has shown to be a supernatural book with its predictive prophecies and amazing consistency, unparalleled manuscript evidence, the power of changed lives, as well as how science and archeology especially have only helped its claims and never hurt them. But I have had many encounters with Jewish people who shared the views of this man, most did not still go to synagogue, did not believe in the reality of their faith, but still considered themselves Jews religiously. There are many people who are Jewish ethnically but do not hold to the beliefs at all. This matters a great deal when we talk with them to know how wide the range can be of varying beliefs.

We read in the Bible that God brought salvation to the world through the Jewish people, and they were the original and only people of the covenant, and then how this was extended to the Gentiles, or non-Jews. The prophet Hosea prophesied of this in the Old Testament, telling of the judgment that would befall Israel to the benefit of the Gentiles in Hosea chapter 2:23,

> *"And I will say to those who were not My people, 'you are My people!' And they will say, 'You are my God."*

The prophet goes on to speak for God to the people and how He will restore them in the future. This is also what the apostle Paul taught about how Israel's judgment from God will be to the benefit of the non-Jews or Gentile people of the world. The Jewish people will be restored though in the future according to Romans chapter 11:17-25. The apostle Paul talks of the Jewish people as the original olive branches that belong on the tree which God had planted. These are the people, these branches, that would be saved and belong to God. He talks of the Gentiles as the wild olive branch, one that was not originally there, but gets grafted on to the same tree. He tells us not to be arrogant toward the branches as well, to never despise or be arrogant toward the Jews because it was through them that salvation came, and the Gentiles were add-ons (see Ephesians 2:12). No one should ever have a mean or condescending attitude toward them for any reason (See Romans 11:17-25).

3

The Shema

I will tell you I miss my family. I still talk with them and get together, but it is not the same. There is a special bond of fellowship that is gone. A certain level of intimacy and closeness that is no longer there, especially with my parents. To some in my family, I am somewhat of a defector I am sure, to others I've just completely lost my mind. They act as if something terrible happened to me like contracting some disease or that I have been duped. But forsaking or denouncing Christ is unthinkable and in terms of persecution, compared to what my brothers and sisters in Christ have faced and still face for professing belief in Jesus, this is nothing.

He is the King of the universe and He is my King and my Savior. He is more important than anyone. I pray for my family's salvation constantly. I pray that God will open their eyes to the salvation that He presents. I ask that you would pray for them also and for others who don't know Christ.

But we can have no other gods before Him as the first commandment tells us, and that God must be worshipped in spirit and in truth (John 4:24).

The Jewish people clung to the most special prayer they had. It was called the Shema, which means "to hear." It relates to the kingship of God, the absolute sovereignty of God for our lives, and our utter love and devotion to Him. Jesus quoted the Shema in Mark 12:28-31 when He was asked what the greatest commandment was.

> *One of the scribes came and heard them arguing, and recognizing that He had answered them well, asked Him, "What commandment is the foremost of all?" Jesus answered, "The foremost is, 'HEAR, O ISRAEL! THE LORD OUR GOD IS ONE LORD; AND YOU SHALL LOVE THE LORD YOUR GOD WITH ALL YOUR HEART, AND WITH ALL YOUR SOUL, AND WITH ALL YOUR MIND, AND WITH ALL YOUR STRENGTH.' "The second is this, 'YOU SHALL LOVE YOUR NIEGHBOR AS YOURSELF.' There is no other commandment greater than these."*

I remember in my youth singing the Shema, the Jewish confession of faith which declares the great truth from Deuteronomy chapter 6:4. The great truth that there is only one God and that He is the Lord over all. It speaks of His power and provision for His people. It reminds us of the total love we are to have for Him, a love that consumes us totally.

"Hear O Israel, the Lord is our God, the Lord is One!"

I remember as I was in the process of writing this book thinking back on how we used to gather together and sing this at temple when we were young. As a kid much of the time I did not want to go to Hebrew School. There were many days when I would argue with my mother about going at the drop off, but it wore off after I was there a while each time, and I always loved the part at the end when we sang this truth, because it made us aware of the awesome majesty of God and made me feel as though we were singing with the very throne God in view. When we sang this, for a few minutes, we were there. As I thought about those moments, pondered them, sitting at the computer writing this book, I stopped typing. I felt as though I was back there singing it again. I sat for a minute and thought about it. I couldn't believe how clear the memory was although I have never recalled this time before. I began to sing it softly, almost as a whisper as I sat at my desk. I hadn't sung it in over thirty years, but remembered the words and that surprised me in a very strange way. As I continued to sing it brought tears to my eyes, and I couldn't finish. I sat there and waited a few minutes before I could go on. The love of God and our love for Him as a result is overwhelming, it should be. Only because He is overwhelming. Overwhelming in love, in power, overwhelming in majesty, and in purity.

You see this displayed in churches that truly give all they have to honor God each week, and just desire to be there, to offer up praise and thanksgiving. They love God so much it just naturally spills out in their worship time. In a situation like this it is never about the people themselves, it is all about Him. Sometimes you see people such as these overwhelmed by the very thought of Him and tears stream down their cheeks, or they have to stop and pause because they can't go on. This is by no means a necessity for God-honoring worship, but it reflects a heart that beats for Him and longs to get to church for corporate worship.

I invite you to go on the internet and find a recording of people singing the Shema corporately in a service and hear the beauty and power of what I am describing.

The Shema was recited by faithful Jews twice a day. After this verse that declares that there is only one God, we are told that we are to love the Lord our God with all of our hearts, with all your souls, and with all of our strength. Jesus told us this as well, saying if you love Me, keep My commandments."

There is no greater love than God's love and it all emanates from Him. Without Him it would not even exist. We love Him because He first loved us, and we need to give Him all that we have to offer.

4

The Tabernacle and the Holiness of God

After God had freed the Hebrew people from Egypt and from Pharaoh, He instructed Moses to build the tabernacle, as told to us in the Book of Exodus (Exodus 25:1-8), to fulfill the promise that God had made, the promise that He would always be with His people, that He would go with them, guiding and protecting them as they went to the Promised Land. The tabernacle was a huge tent that God had the Israelite people construct for the worship of God, to which He gave Moses explicit instructions with exact specifications. Each task in building and serving in the tabernacle was done by specific tribes assigned by God to do so with very specific instructions.

The people would camp in a circle around it, arranged by tribe. This was what God had them construct for worship because they were a semi-nomadic people and would be traveling until they reached the Promised Land. This way they could take it down when they had to move on and put it back up when they arrived to the place where they would be camped. At this point in the history of Israel they couldn't have a permanent temple for worship. This could not happen until they reached the Promised Land, the land that the Lord had promised, the land of milk and honey as it is described. This land encompassed modern day Israel and extended beyond her modern borders. In the future when the Israelite nation did get the land God promised them, they did indeed have temples to worship the Lord, including the one that Solomon built to replace the tabernacle, and later Herod's temple in Jerusalem. Jesus, however, prophesied of a time that was coming when true worshippers would not go to a temple to worship the Father (John 4:23), there would no location where access to God was available only, and that only by the priests of the day. Jesus told of a day when believers would worship God in spirit and in truth (John4:24). Believers would no longer be defined by the location of where they worshiped, but by what was in the heart worshiping God through the Son. He was speaking of the cross which was to come and would accomplish the wonderful access to the throne of God that He would create. God's Spirit would dwell in His very people.

But by studying what it was like at the time of the tabernacle you understand the unimagined access we now have to God. In addition, most importantly, we gain an understanding of the magnitude of who He is, and we see the separation that exists between us and God because He is altogether holy and we are not. We learn about His perfect character. Back in the times of the Exodus and the journey to the Promised Land, the relationship with God was not by any means casual, there was great separation and formality. Simply because God was physically manifested to them, the people could not just waltz in and be before Him, or just casually hang out with God. There was a great separation between the two that we need to grasp. This was not done simply because of any arbitrary formality or just some display of power but was only due to the magnitude of separation between us and God. By our nature in comparison to God, without Christ that separation is still there. God is still perfectly holy while we are still not. This is why the chasm exists. If it were not for the righteousness of Christ applied to us as believers we would never be able to stand in God's presence ever. No one could be in His immediate presence and live. It would be too much for anyone.

If you were around back then and happened to stumble upon the nation of Israel in the desert, you would have seen the people camped around the large tent structure with a barrier surrounding it all the way around. This fence-like structure contains the curtains of the tabernacle's outer court. This went all the way around and prevented anyone from even seeing the tabernacle from outside. This marked the separation of the outside world from the splendor that was with them in the tabernacle itself.

So there was this barrier, like a fence that surrounded the tabernacle, with pillars separating the curtains that blocked any view, made to exact specifications that God gave to Moses, made of acacia wood, with bronze posts at the base of each. It must have been striking seeing the curtains made of fine, pure, white linen, closing off the desert from the tabernacle, symbolizing the separation from an unholy and sin-stained and tainted world.

Something immediately came to mind when I was writing about this. We once had a major snowstorm on Long Island when I was growing up. We lived in an old and beautiful neighborhood. The streets were centuries old, windy, hilly, and tree covered. The storm had occurred later in the day, after everyone had already gone home, and the snow had blanketed the landscape completely and was totally untouched and very deep. It had come quickly and completely shut everything down. People just wanted to settle in and wait it out. They could begin to deal with it tomorrow. They knew they were going nowhere at the moment.

The snow had stopped falling around nightfall and at this point had left nothing uncovered. There was a perfect thick blanket of snow over the entire scene. Every tree, every house, every bit of ground, all were left completely immaculate. Nobody was around, it was totally quiet. It was like the snow muffled any sound that was there. I still think about it to this day and wish I could go back. The moon was out and lit the whole scene, its light reflecting off the snow, making it glisten. I felt as though I stumbled upon a massive vault of precious gems as far as I could see. It is still the closest thing I have seen to flawless in my life. As I walked along, the contours of the scene changed but it still remained crystalline white, pristine, pure. I just wanted to keep going the beauty was so alluring. The contrast was amazing between what was there before and what was there now. It wasn't the same anymore. The whole landscape was transformed. It was now unblemished, clean, and completely quiet, it was surreal.

When I first saw it and came out of the house, I walked out slowly, captivated by the scene, taking it all in. There was not another person in sight. Every step was muffled by the blanket of snow, on the ground and on the trees. I have been in snow covered landscapes since but nothing has compared to the level of beauty and peace that I walked through that night. I walked around through the streets as long as I could, not wanting to leave it. If the beauty of this world reflects the glory of God as the Scriptures tell us it does, we have to take the most exemplary scene and display of glory here and multiply it by a quantity beyond us to reach the glory that must be in heaven. Our state of glorification by God is necessary to be able to handle the magnitude of what we'll be in the presence of.

The complete glory of God is so radiant, so dazzling, that as even the moonlight off of the snow made me gasp, His glory would clearly be too much for me, for anyone! This is what the curtains of the tabernacle symbolize. You're in this barren, stark, harsh desert world, and then you walk up to the tabernacle and bam! It is analogous to my feeling walking out of my house that night after the storm. I was indoors, heard the storm was over, heard about the record snowfall. So naturally I opened the door from the darkened house and saw the scene outside, and it hit me, and I gasped, "Wow!" I lost a breath. That is the difference between God and us. The pristine white of the linen, of the curtains of the tabernacle, representing God's holiness, contrasting the rugged and drab landscape of the desert, saying to us, "We are exiting the un-pure, the tainted nature of this world, and are now moving into the midst of something beyond us and our capabilities, other-worldly, the realm of the holy, the realm where God Himself dwells. The Holy of Holies, the King of Kings, un-compromised beauty and wonder. In studying the Tabernacle and especially inside the tent which houses the Holy of Holies and God's very presence, learning about them makes you realize that it is utterly unthinkable to imagine someone just strolling in casually to this place where God dwells, or going there at all! We will be like Job when God appeared to him in a whirlwind. Job told God of how he had heard about Him but upon seeing Him realized He is so much more than Job ever could have imagined (Job 42:5-6).

> *I have heard of You by the hearing of the ear; but now my eye sees You; therefore I retract, and I repent in dust and ashes."*

Beyond the curtains was the Outer Court; in it were the laver, a large basin made of bronze, used for ceremonial cleansing of the priests, to prepare to minister there to the Lord, as well as the altar used for sacrifices which all pointed to the perfect sacrifice of Christ which was to come. The priests had to go through elaborate cleansing rites to prepare to be before the Lord. They could never make themselves good enough by these rituals, it was only that the Lord ordained them and found them acceptable. There was a door that separated anyone from entering into even the Outer Court. Only people presenting sacrifices could enter the court. Only the Priests could minister in the tabernacle itself, where the presence of the Lord was manifest.

Then there was another door blocking entrance into the tent, the house of God. Inside the tent the first room was called the Holy Place. This contained the Golden Lampstand, the Table of Showbread, and the Altar of Incense. All of these structures were covered with gold and the holy place was adorned with tapestries on the walls in a beautiful array of colors. The Lampstand was a seven candled menorah, which was kept permanently lit in the Holy Place and prefigured Christ who was to come, who is the Light of the world. Jesus said,

> "I am the light of the world, he who follows Me shall not walk in darkness, but shall have the light of life" (John 8:12).

F.F. Bruce articulated how Jesus is the embodiment of the language of the Hebrew Scriptures. He cannot be separated from the degree of involvement He possesses in it.

> "In the OT God is his people's light (Psalm 27:1); in the light of his presence they enjoy grace and peace (Numbers 6:24-26). The Servant of the Lord is appointed as a light to the nations, so that God's salvation may extend to the end of the earth (Isaiah 49:6). The word or law of God is also described as a light to guide the path of the obedient (Psalm 119:105; Proverbs 6:23). So Jesus, as the Son of the Father, the Servant of the Lord and the Word incarnate, embodies the OT language. Even before the Word became incarnate, the life

which he eternally possessed, says John, "was the light of men (John 1:4); now by his incarnation the true light has come into the world, providing illumination for all (John 1:9; 3:19)."[1]

God is the source of all light. In heaven we are told that there will be no sun, for the glory of the Lord will illumine the landscape brilliantly.

"And the city has no need of the sun or of the moon to shine upon it, for the glory of the God has illuminated it, and its lamp is the Lamb" (Revelation 21:31).

To not walk in the light leaves only walking in darkness. This light that Jesus describes of Himself is the same that was described in the Old Testament by the Psalmist who said,

"For with You is the fountain of life; in Your light we see light" (Psalm 36:9).

Jesus is the source of light that shows us the path to life which only can lead to Him.

The showbread displayed on the table of Showbread is to symbolize the perfect provision by God for His people. There were twelve loaves to symbolize the twelve tribes of Israel. This prefigures Christ as well who proclaimed the vital union with Him that was necessary for eternal life, that He was the Bread of life and that anyone who comes to Him would never hunger in John chapter 6:35. At that time, people were missing this point when Jesus was teaching this truth and miraculously feeding them, and were looking to be filled for the moment. Jesus knew that they needed to focus beyond this life to the spiritual, and that this permanent need could only be found in Him and it would last forever.

Also in the Holy Place the Golden Altar of Incense which gave the entire tabernacle a fragrant aroma as all sacrifices that were pleasing to God were described as a fragrant aroma to God. The greatest and most

---

[1] The Gospel & The Epistles of John, F.F. Bruce, 188

pleasing of all aromas to God the Father was that of the Son, in His perfect sacrifice. The Altar of Incense had a golden crown upon the top of it which signifies "Jesus, crowned with glory and honor" (Hebrews 2:9). The burning incense signified prayer, prayer rising up to the throne of God. Jesus modeled the central importance of prayer for our lives during His ministry on earth as God incarnate. He was constantly in prayer, and we need to follow this model which teaches to discover our true and utter dependence upon God.

God calls us to prayer in our worship of Him and also to fulfill our needs from our Creator.

This awakens us to our reliance upon Him, and He is glorified all the more, for we would have nothing without Him. And when we pray according to the will of God as is displayed in Scripture, this is pleasing to Him, which is our greatest ambition (2 Corinthians 5:9).

As we move into the structure of the Tabernacle the intensity of beauty and adornment increases as you move closer to the presence of God. The curtains increase in beauty and the objects are of even greater prominence. William Brown's book *The Tabernacle, Its Priests and its Services,* is a book that does a wonderful job of describing the physical nature of the tabernacle, but even more importantly the reverent nature of the significance of the tabernacle. The significance of it all lies solely due to the nature of the One whose presence dwells there. The book is so commendable because besides presenting an accurate portrait of the dimensions and functions of the tabernacle, it does not leave out the most important element, that of God Himself.

> "Leaving the first apartment of the tabernacle and its lovely and richly ornamented vessels, the table of Shewbread, the seven branched candlestick and altar of incense behind, we now pass beyond the veil, and enter the most holy place, the throne room of Israel's God and King. Let us approach with deepest reverence, put off our shoes, for if any place surely this we now tread is holy ground. It outshone in splendor the holy place, one of whose walls, the east one, forming the door, had no cherubim displayed on it; but, as we have already seen, every

one of the four walls and roof of the most holy place, was resplendent with blue, purple, scarlet and bright shining cherubim, and besides those glowing on roof and walls, two of solid gold stood on the mercy seat."[2]

After leaving the holy place we reach the place which captured my imagination more than any single concept in my growth as a young Jewish boy. It was a place even my dreams could not capture. In my mind the concept of whose presence dwells inside draws a blank. This happened in my mind because I could not conjure up or draw on any analogy that could contain or explain it.

Also, to try and do so would be an attempt to capture God, as well it would be a graven image of the One that we are never to do or desire to. This was the most sacred place on earth at the time. This place separated from all people, the place that lay beyond the Holy Place, separated by the curtain preventing entrance, this was the Holy of Holies.

This was the place where the ark of the covenant was kept, where the manifestation of God Himself dwelled. This area in the Tabernacle was so special, so holy, and for good reason and only for one reason. It was regarded as such just as the spot in the Midianite wilderness was regarded as holy when Moses met God. He was told to take the sandals off his feet because the ground where he stood was holy ground. Why was that? This was because Almighty God, El Shaddai, "The One Who Thunders" was there.

In the Holy of Holies the presence of God was made manifest for the people of Israel. No one could ever step foot in that place and live. It was unthinkable to even consider it.

Once a year the high priest only would enter. He would enter on the holiest day of the year, Yom Kippur, the Day of Atonement. He would sprinkle blood on the mercy seat, the cover of the Ark of the Covenant, representing the throne of God. It was a type of the very throne of the Lord in heaven.

The priest presented this sacrifice to God for the sins of the people. This had to be repeated every year, year after year. This was acceptable

---

[2] The Tabernacle, Its Priests and Its Services, William Brown, 73

to God as it pointed to the one perfect sacrifice to come, the one that would take away the sins of the people completely and permanently, forever. The perfect sacrifice of the Savior, the Messiah, Jesus Christ our Lord. The Book of Hebrews spends much time describing this to us and the superiority of Christ over everything else. We learn there of the superiority of His sacrifice over these old sacrifices made by the priests for the people, that had to be repeated over and over, because they were not perfect, and how the sacrifice of Christ never had to be repeated because it attained its intended purpose, obtaining eternal redemption for those who believe (Hebrews 1:1-14; 10:14).

The priest could only go into the Holy of Holies once a year, and as we have seen was separated from the rest of the tabernacle, and from the adjoining Holy Place by a very thick folded curtain. This separated the people from God's presence. This is what was split in two when Jesus completed His work on the cross. This was a great symbol of the redemptive event on the cross. We then have access to the throne of God! Amazing. Raised as a Jew I feel the weight of that, the utter privilege. Study the Book of Hebrews and when you're done you'll say, "Now I know why Matt was so excited by the New Covenant, and by what we now have in Christ." Dive into it and it will change your life, as will the rest of Scripture.

Some are listening to how elaborate and specified the building of the Tabernacle had to be, or the sacred nature of the Holy Place and Holy of Holies, and may be thinking, "What's all the fuss about?" First off, I must say, when I hear statements like that, before I can even answer, I have to pause, I have to wait. I first physically feel the weight of such a thing. I can almost feel myself sway backward. I need a moment to recover from it. Then I give a response and pray the person through the grace of God sees the folly in that. I have also heard the comment, "All that was just for the Old Covenant, and has no meaning now." The answer is that although much has changed due to the work of Christ on our behalf, nothing has changed in regards to the perfect character and majesty of God. We lose sight of who we are dealing with, and that's when only such misconceptions are possible. When this happens we are then out of touch with His holy nature and in an awful place.

In our affairs here on earth we even have an expectation of formality for certain people of certain rank and stature. Think of the pomp and circumstance to even approaching an earthly king in the ancient world? Look at what even surrounds our own President and other world leaders? We remember the royal wedding in England between Princess Diana and Charles, the coronation of the Queen, we remember all that was involved there. Why do we do this? Why do why accept it, or see it as fitting? It is because this level of respect and ceremony is all in relation to the degree of the office that is held. Think of a judge in the courtroom. His bench is high, he wears a robe, we dress nicely when we're in his presence, when we talk to him we call him "Your honor." He does also have the power to throw us in jail, but seriously we do this because of the degree of the office that is held. And we need to remember that there is no true comparison for the differences in office held by God due to His nature of perfection and that of man. These analogies in our world are helpful and aid us in our understanding, but in God's case all hopelessly break down at some point because He is so much greater to anything that we can we compare to Him.

Isaiah chapter 40:18 says,

> *"To whom then will you liken God? Or what likeness will you compare with Him?"*

Or in chapter 55:8 of the same book God says,

> *"For My thoughts are not your thoughts, nor are your ways My ways," declares the Lord. "For as the heavens are higher than the earth, so are My ways higher than your ways and My thoughts than your thoughts."*

Hosea 11:9 God says,

> *"For I am God and not man, the Holy One in your midst."*

I remember being invited to an event and was not informed that it was very formal, black tie only. We of course showed up dressed very casually. It was awful. We felt like slobs, exposed, and as though we weren't wearing anything at all. We felt like we rudely crashed the party and were never invited. I remember some people were insulted that we did that, but we didn't know. But it didn't help, we couldn't wait to get out of there. The people who were there weren't snobs, we did look disrespectful. I felt that way and we're talking human beings to human beings, sinners to sinners. What about compared to a perfect spotless being? Our sin would make us feel more than naked, or much worse than rude, it would all be brought out in front of us, we would feel it tangibly, feel the difference between us and God. Compared to perfection, to the absolutely flawless, we would disintegrate just like Isaiah did in chapter six of the book of his name (Isaiah 6:1-7). When I walked outside to that undisturbed scene after the snowstorm I described earlier, into that purity, I know once I did it would never be the same. I knew there was no way I couldn't enter into it without disturbing it, tainting it. Thank God through faith in Christ we can be covered with His righteousness we are accepted and can then walk into heaven and not taint it at all.

When God gave the Law to the people, they could not draw into His immediate presence.

In Exodus chapter 19 the people had to prepare for this most royal event. Again this preparation has to do with our inability to be in the His presence of God because as we saw with Isaiah, He is holy and we are not (Exodus 19:10). In Exodus 19 God prepares the people to meet with Him to receive the Law. They must prepare for the most solemn assembly possible for their lives. The people had to be taught the magnitude of who God is, and then they will be able to see the magnitude of His Law, this Law that reflects His perfect character. We will never be able to comprehend the gravity of breaking it if we don't have a grasp for the sacred One it represents. We are not holy and can compromise holiness and righteousness, God cannot. This is the first step to understanding God and why humanity is in the predicament it is in, is in the holiness of the God and of the Law which is a natural outflow of His moral perfection.

In verse 10,

> *The Lord also said to Moses, "Go to the people and consecrate them today and tomorrow, and let them wash*

their garments; and let them be ready for the third day, for on the third day the Lord will come down on Mount Sinai in the sight of all the people. You shall set bounds for the people all around, saying, "Beware that you do not go up on the mountain or touch the border of it; whoever touches the mountain shall surely be put to death. No hand shall touch him, but he shall surely be stoned or shot through; whether beast or man, he shall not live. When the rams horn sounds a long blast, they shall come up to the mountain. So Moses went down from the mountain to the people and consecrated the people, and they washed their garments. He said to the people, be ready for the third day; do not go near a woman. So it came about on the third day, when it was morning, that there were thunder and lightning flashes and a thick cloud upon the mountain and a very loud trumpet sound, so that all the people who were in the camp trembled. And Moses brought the people out of the camp to meet God, and they stood at the foot of the mountain. Now Mount Sinai was all in smoke because the Lord descended upon it in fire; and its smoke ascended like the smoke of a furnace and the whole mountain quaked violently. When the sound of the trumpet grew louder and louder, Moses spoke and God answered him with thunder. The Lord came down on Mount Sinai, to the top of the mountain, and Moses went up.

The second time Moses came back down from the mountain and from his meeting with God, his face shown bright from being near the glory of the Lord. Moses had asked God to show Him His face while on Sinai with Him, but God told him that Moses could not survive this. So God let him see but a small portion of glory after He lovingly placed Moses safely in the cleft of a rock for protection and covered him. God slowly passed by and let Moses see a portion of Him, a backward glance (Exodus 33:18-23. When Moses came back down from Mt. Sinai after meeting with God again, his face shown brightly, it glowed from but a mere exposure to the Lord of Glory. The people were afraid however, and made him cover his face (Exodus 34:29-33).

We need to remember these moments and never forget them, never becoming casual about God. If we pour through the Scriptures we can't miss it, it's everywhere. As an aside, look at your Bible and see how much of it is Old Testament, and think about how much God-breathed revelation we miss out on if we ignore it. God is patient and loving toward us, that's why we still exist. Let us not insult His holiness and disdain His love and mercy with lackadaisical worship, casual, flippant, or selfish prayer, or no desire to learn more about Him in His Word. No wonder we grow afraid of circumstances and live many times in fear of living or of dying, or get deceived by strange and destructive doctrines because we don't fully know who He is, and are not subsequently changed by it. I have had people come to me and tell that they can't help but worry a lot, seemingly about everything. They say how they hate living with the anxiety day to day. This again stems from our not knowing Him as we should. We will always struggle more with this kind of faith, but the more we study Him in His Word the less we will be in that anxiety. I include myself in this and need to work on this as much as anyone. The longer we live and we experience His love and faithfulness, the more he keeps growing, and getting bigger and bigger until we look up and are enveloped in wonder. In another scene from the Old Testament we see a time when Moses couldn't take the complaining of his fellow people anymore as they wandered through the desert. They were ungratefully complaining because they had been eating manna in the wilderness for so long after being rescued from Egypt and wanted meat to eat, so he called to God for help. God told Moses He would give them meat to eat. Moses asked how could this be possible because there were so many thousands people? After all he had seen of the great works of God He didn't know how God could do it. The Lord answered Moses with a statement that when I repeat I can't help but say with a level of excitement. God asked Moses, "Is the Lord's power limited?" (Numbers 11:23). Had something happened to the power of the Almighty He was asking? The answer is of course no, and then God provided meat for everyone. God is as magnificent now as He was then and will do the same for you.

Growing up Jewish you are immersed in stories like these, and over and over it paints the picture of the enormity and greatness of our God. In Hebrew school we studied these magnificent portrayals of God in the Psalms, as the Creator, as the ultimate Sovereign of the universe. All the Bible is of course inspired by God, but we can't let ourselves miss the grand presentations of God in the Old Testament. Psalm 8 is a great example. As you read this next passage, think of Jesus, God incarnate, walking the earth healing people as they cried out to Him. Think of Him showing the extent of His love for us. Or recite this the next time you look up at a starry nighttime sky. Psalm 8:1,3) says,

> *"O Lord, our Lord, how majestic is Your name in all the earth, Who have displayed Your splendor above the heavens!*
> *When I consider Your heavens, the work of Your fingers, the moon and the stars, which You have ordained; what is man that You take thought of him, and the son of man that care for him?"*

We have lost sight of who God is. I am troubled by what I see and hear. Where is the reverence and awe for God, for His majesty? As we said previously, it is because we don't study Him and His character enough as presented to us in the Bible. We grow dull and unappreciative without it. We go through the rituals of faith, instead of in amazement over Him. We plod along, instead of being on fire to learn about Him, to grow in our knowledge of Him, and to serve Him. This knowledge is the only way to reach the deeper stages of our love and service for God. How can you get closer to someone, more intimate, without knowing them better and better all the time? That is what intimacy is all about. This also comes from a strong and vital prayer life and from obedience to Him which will bring the subsequent blessing of further intimacy with Him.

David, called a man after God's own heart, said in Psalm 119:9-16,

> *"How can a young man keep his way pure? By keeping it according to Your word. With all my heart I have sought*

You; do not let me wander from Your commandments. Your word I have treasured in my heart, that I might not sin against You. With my lips I have told of all the ordinances of Your mouth. I have rejoiced in the way of Your testimonies, as much as in all riches. I will meditate on Your precepts and regard Your ways. I shall delight in Your statutes; I shall not forget Your word."

Do we feel that way about the Word? Jesus, speaking of the Bible, said, "Man does not feed by bread alone, but on every word that proceeds out of the mouth of God" (Matthew 4:4). We should be consumed with God, so much so that we are seeking His word as a lost and starving man crawling in the desert looks for something to eat. As Jews the respect was such for the Word that all would rise during a service at temple as His Word was removed from the place where it was held, hidden from view. The Torah, the first five books of the Bible, the books of Moses, were on large scrolls, written in Hebrew, and covered with a beautiful, ornate covering. The Rabbi would touch it and bring his fingers to his lips and kiss them.

We should regard His name in the same way. The Jewish people saw the name of God as so holy that they would not even write His name. This is the name God gave to Moses in the desert when he asked God at the burning bush who to say sent him before going to Egypt (Exodus 3:14). The name God said would be a memorial to all generations. The ineffable name of God. No one would dare write it down lest they felt it would violate one of the Great Commandments of God, that of taking the Lord's name in vain. This is how sacred it was to them. It was not sacred because they held it to be sacred, or because they had made Him their deity. It was sacred because of the nature of the One it belonged to. How far away have we come from that today? Three of the top ten laws that God gave His people involved how we worship Him. Laws which Jesus Himself upheld and gave to us.

Although as believers in Him we are free from the Law and its condemnation, our hearts beat to fulfill them after we are saved out of love for God and what He values, these values subsumed by these Laws.

Number one, having no other gods before Him, the worship of other false gods is prohibited. This is first, this is because there are no others, no other Gods, and to worship supposed others would be worshiping a lie, and God hates falsehood as He has said that He is a God of Truth.

Second, no creating of idols in His place, today that could mean anything we place in front of God in importance. Think of all of things we worship and value ahead of God; ourselves, money, fame, status, power, cars, famous people, athletes, and on and on.

Third, using the Lord's name in vain. If you possessed your own island and was going to start a country of your own, and began a system of government, what would your top ten laws be? Would you have any of these as the top three? I ask myself this same question. These are the top three for God. We'd all probably have one for murder and one for theft. But would any pertain to the worship of God? This is really something for all of us to spend time pondering.

We went to Orlando for vacation one time and we found a place that we didn't even know existed. It was called the Holy Land Experience. For those who have never been there, I recommend it. It was built by Zion's Hope Ministries. They have reconstructed a replica of part of the city of Jerusalem, with the gates and everything. Everyone is dressed authentically, it was really great. They even have a beautiful six story replica of the Jewish Temple King Herod built. It takes you back in time to what it would be like walking around ancient Jerusalem, and being there before the destruction of the temple in A.D. 70. I thought of this, of our Lord, the Lord Jesus, the Creator of heaven and earth, standing before this temple and saying that in three days if this temple was destroyed He could rebuild it (John 2:19). He was speaking about His resurrection, but if He wanted to He could certainly destroy it with but a word and rebuild it just the same.

I stood there and thought of how the original was built to worship Him and then He was being rejected standing right in front of it. Wow.

Earlier that day I was waiting for my wife who was in a shop there and noticed a sign beside a tree. When I walked over to it I saw it was an acacia tree, the same type God had instructed Moses to use to build the Tabernacle, the tent of meeting and worship of God, where God's presence would be with them, and also use this wood for the construction of the Ark of the Covenant. It also had the corresponding verses from Scripture on a plaque by the tree. I read them and just stared up at that tree. I took it in, thinking of the greatness of God, was lost in it for a moment, and without realizing, had tears streaming down my face.

My wife came out and asked me what was wrong as I was still looking up at it. I explained it to her and she smiled. Then she said, "What would ever happen if we ever got to go to the real Holy Land, You'd be a wreck!"

The God of the Old Testament and of the New Testament are the same. The God who thundered on Sinai, parted the sea, had the giant fish swallow up Jonah, and then spit Him out safely on shore, who sent down fire from heaven on Mt Carmel proving that the gods of the prophets of Baal were no gods at all. This is the same God to whom the Bible says (Ps. 104:1-4, 31-21),

> "Bless the Lord O my soul! O my God, You are very great; You are clothed with splendor and majesty, covering Yourself with light as a cloak, stretching out heaven like a tent curtain. He lays the beams of His upper chambers in the waters; He makes the clouds His chariot; He walks upon the wings of the wind; He makes the winds His messengers, flaming fire His ministers.
>
> Let the glory of the Lord endure forever; let the Lord be glad in His works; He looks at the earth and it trembles; He touches the mountains, and they smoke"

This is the same God who calmed the raging storm on the boat as the apostles watched in fear and wonder, who with but the power of His Word said, *"Be still."* This is the same Word that when He spoke the entire universe was created, and when He commanded *"Lazarus, come forth,"* the dead rose. This is all the same God. For there is only one and He does not change (Malachi 3:6)

5

It's The Most Christian Thing I Could Do

> ..."If anyone else has mind to put confidence in the flesh, I far more: circumcised the eighth day, of the nation of Israel, of the tribe of Benjamin, a Hebrew of Hebrews; as to the Law, A Pharisee. But whatever things were gain to me, those things I have counted as loss for the sake of Christ." Philippians 3:4,5,7

As I mentioned most people seem so surprised at my professing to be a follower of Christ because I am Jewish. To them it is such a stretch from my background. In reality, it is the most natural thing for a Jewish person to do. The Old Testament contains three quarters of the story of our redemption by God, but Christianity (in the New Testament) is a consummation of the story, a fulfillment. Jesus Himself said in Matthew 5:17:

> "Do not think that I came to abolish the Law or the Prophets; I did not come to abolish but to fulfill."

The terms Law and the Prophets refer to the Old Testament. Jesus was clearly saying that He is here to fulfill all of the Old Testament. He wanted everyone to know that in no way would He be in violation of all that the Old Testament was about. It is part of God's Word, and Jesus is deity, so it is His Word. He goes on in the next verse to expand on this. In verse 18:

> *"For truly I say to you, until heaven and earth pass away, not the smallest letter or stroke shall pass away from the Law until all is accomplished."*

Again, when Jesus refers to the Law. He is talking about what makes up the Old Testament, and that all of it must accomplished, fulfilled, even down to the smallest element of it. Putting that smallest element into contemporary terms would be the dot of an "i" or the cross of a "t." So Christianity is in no way a new or unique faith apart from biblical Judaism, it is the completion of it as was predicted by God Himself. The apostle Paul also made this point right off the bat in the beginning of his epistle to the Romans, writing in chapter one, verses 1 and 2, that not only is he called by God Himself to preach this gospel, but also that this message of good news, of salvation, was the very same one promised to the forefathers all through the Old Testament, by the prophets who spoke from God.

The apostle Paul who penned that opening statement is the quintessential example of all I am talking about here in this book (Romans 1;1-2).

> *Paul, a bond-servant of Christ Jesus, called as an apostle, set apart for the gospel of God, which He promised beforehand through the prophets in the Holy Scriptures.*

The apostle, under the inspiration of the Holy Spirit, wanted to be sure that people understood, especially the Jewish people of his time that this is no new doctrine which is opposed to the writings and teachings of Moses. On the contrary, Paul here is saying that it is the very consummation of a mystery that he describes was hidden in the Old Testament, promised, thinly veiled, and now, by God's grace, revealed. That is the message of the apostle then that was from God, and that is the same message we are to convey today, the good news, or gospel of Jesus Christ.

The first presentation of the gospel came in the book of Genesis. In chapter 3 of the book of Genesis, in verse 15, God declared to the serpent (the devil):

> *"And I will put enmity between you and the woman, and between your offspring and hers; He will crush your head, and you will strike His heel."*

This is a description of what Jesus will do to Satan, He will crush him and Satan will only strike at the Messiah's heel. This was the first pronouncement of God's plan of salvation. Romans 5:12 sums it up for us:

> *Therefore, just as through one man sin entered into the world, and death through sin, and so death spread to all men, because all sinned.*

Adam was God's infallible choice to act on behalf of the human race in the garden. Adam was our federal head, our representative. What he chose to do impacted every generation of human beings for the entire course of human history. So through Adam's sin, sin was introduced in the world and death along with it as it says in Romans 6:23:

> *For the wages of sin is death, but the free gift of God is eternal life in Christ Jesus our Lord.*

So the penalty of sin is death, and as Romans 5:12 says it spread to all men because all, every one of us, has sinned. But so good is the news that follows that there is forgiveness through Jesus Christ. Sin is the problem, death is the result, and Jesus is the solution.

So God announces the gospel first in Genesis 3. In Genesis chapter 15 we learn how we receive that salvation-it is by faith (Genesis 15:6). Abraham, who God used to form the Jewish nation, received the promise of God that all of the nations of the world would be blessed through his seed. This blessing would occur by the Messiah. The Messiah would come to redeem the world through his family line. Abraham had only an idea of what this would look like, of exactly how this promise would be manifested, but he believed God, he had faith in what God told him, he trusted God and the salvation he offers, which was credited to him as righteousness. God would see him as righteous. He was saved at that point and would then spend an eternity with God. When we put our faith in Christ as our Savior, we are trusting in Him for our redemption, not ourselves. If we try to do this without God, trusting in our own goodness, this will never measure up. We cannot ever measure up to God's standard of righteousness, and cannot even be in the presence of a holy God. Our God cannot even look upon evil (Habakkuk 1:13), and our best deeds, our own righteousness, is like filthy rags compared to God's righteousness (Isaiah 64:6). That is why Christ came, to seek and to save the lost (Luke 19:10; 1 Timothy 1:15). God came and did what we could not do for ourselves, live a life according to God's perfect standard, and give that righteousness that was His to those who believe. So by believing in Him, His righteousness is given to us.

Romans 5 continues to sum up the whole history of man's relationship with God and what the Messiah accomplished for us in Romans 5:17-19:

> *For if by the transgression of the one, death reigned through the one, much more those who receive the abundance of grace and of the gift of righteousness will reign in life through the One, Jesus Christ. So then as through one transgression there resulted condemnation to all men, even so through one act of righteousness there resulted justification of life to all men. For as through one man's disobedience the many were made sinners, even so through the obedience of the One the many will be made righteous.*

And the Messiah also paid the price for our sins on the cross satisfying the demands of divine justice to which we deserved.

> *When you were dead in your transgressions and the uncircumcision of the flesh, He made you alive together with Him, having forgiven us all our transgressions, having canceled out the certificate of debt consisting of decrees against us, which was hostile to us; and He has taken it out of the way, having nailed it to the cross.* (Colossians 2:13-14)

So from the garden to the promise made to Abraham, God's plan of redemption for His people was unfolding. Everything from the Exodus, to the wandering in the desert, the sacrifices made to God, all prefigured the One who was to come, the Messiah.

This story of redemption begins in the first book of the Bible, and is consummated in the last book of the Bible, Revelation. The fulfillment of Old Testament prophecies, namely Jesus, has already arrived, and will return again, for the final chapter of human history (2 Thessalonians 1:7-9; 1 Thessalonians 4:13-18; 2 Peter 3:3-13).

So we can see how there should be no surprise to people who are familiar with the story of redemption as presented in the Bible, and not see some illogical leap from Judaism to Christianity. Christianity is the fulfillment of the Old Testament. God put His supernatural mark on these events. He confirmed His spokesman in the Scriptures through miracles, authenticating their words by these demonstrations of His power. Jesus said in Matthew 12 verse 28:

> *"But I cast out demons by the Spirit of God, then the kingdom of God has come upon you."*

The miracles Jesus performed were to prove who He was, that He was God in the flesh, come here to save His people from their sins as the Old Testament promised the Messiah would. They prove, or give testimony of who He was, sent from heaven as the Savior of the world. This again, is what every Jew longed for, growing up reading about in the sacred Scriptures.

And in John 5:36:

> *"But the testimony which I have is greater than the testimony of John (the Baptist); for the works which the Father has given Me to accomplish-the very works I do-testify about Me, that the Father has sent Me."*

He goes on to say on verse 37 and 38:

> *"And the Father who sent Me, He has testified of Me. You have neither heard His voice at any time nor seen*

His form. You do not have His word abiding in you, for you do not believe Him whom He sent."

Out of all of the miracles that verify that Jesus is who He said He was, the greatest was that of His resurrection. Jesus claimed to be the Messiah, He claimed to be God, and He proved it through His rising from the dead. As well He showed wisdom that amazed people, and spoke with an authority they had never seen. When the Pharisees sent the guards to bring Him (Jesus) back to them, they returned empty-handed. When they arrived without Him, they asked why He was not with them. They answered that no man speaks as this man does. It was not the time for Him, the Son of Man, to be delivered up into the hands of His enemies, which He voluntarily allowed (John 10:11,15,18). This was prophesied by the prophets in the Old Testament, and had to be consummated for Scripture to be fulfilled and for any of us to be saved (Matthew 16:21; Matthew 26:53-56). This was seen through the signs and wonders, the miracles Jesus performed. But the most undeniable proof again came in His resurrection which we cover later in this book.

God promised and predicted all of these events in the Old Testament. We will deal with all of these claims and prophecies in the chapter on the Messiah and all of the prophecies connected with His appearing, but for the sake of demonstrating the flow in the Bible we will present some here. The prophet Isaiah predicted the coming Messiah, and through him God tells us much about what He will be like and how He will enter into the world. In Isaiah chapter 7 verse 14 says:

Therefore the Lord Himself will give you a sign: Behold, a virgin will be with child and bear a son, and she will call His name Immanuel.

This prophecy was of course fulfilled in the New Testament, with Mary as the mother, and being a virgin bearing a son. We all have heard the story, but do we see it as a direct fulfillment of Old Testament prophecy? Matthew 1:23 tells us that the name Immanuel means God with us, the birth of Christ, the coming of the Messiah signaled a great bursting through of the kingdom of God upon our planet. The historic conclusion of God's promises in the Old Testament, was long awaited by every Jew who believed. Isaiah chapter 9 goes on to describe the coming Messiah further. We learn more about who He will be and what He will be like. This is God's unmistakable signature on the Messiah. This way there will be no doubt as to the authenticity of the Messiah and also no doubt as to who He really is. Isaiah 9:6-7:

> *For a child will be born to us, a son will be given to us; and the government will rest on His shoulders; and His name will be called Wonderful Counselor, Mighty God, Eternal Father, Prince of Peace. There will be no end to the increase of His government or of peace, on the throne of David and over His kingdom, to establish it and to uphold it with justice and righteousness from then on and forever more. The zeal of the Lord of hosts will accomplish this.*

So at this point the marvelous flow of the story of our redemption, of God's mighty and merciful work on our behalf is seen. Jesus is the central figure, and deservedly so. The Old Testament is loaded with imagery of Christ and His atoning death. The book of Hebrews, in the New Testament, goes to great lengths to demonstrate this connection, which is discussed at length in the chapter, My Burden for My People. But we see again how belief in Jesus is not only natural if you hold to the Old Testament, it is inescapable. Jesus is everywhere in the Old Testament, the ceremonies of the Old Testament are representations, symbols and shadows of what was to come, and what was fulfilled in the New Testament. Again, the book of Hebrews labors to bring this point home (Hebrews 10:4-13).

The prophet Micah of the Old Testament was used to prophecy of where the Messiah will be born in Micah 5:2:

> *But as for you, Bethlehem Ephrathah, too little to be among the clans of Judah, from you One will go forth for Me to be ruler in Israel. His goings forth are from long ago, from the days of eternity.*

The flow from the Old Testament to the New Testament is natural and inevitable. The New Testament also has the same marks of divinity as does the Old. When the apostles wrote of the Scriptures of the New Testament they called them God breathed, inspired (2 Timothy 3:16). This was written referring to the Old Testament, which Jesus also called God speaking to us (Matthew 22:31), and that the Scripture cannot be broken (John 10:35), Jesus was saying that we have to accept it all as authoritative, not just parts of it. But the apostles also refer to the New Testament writing as Scripture as well. In Peter's second letter (2nd Peter in the New Testament, (2 Peter 3:15-16), he wrote in chapter 3 verses 15 and 16 about the writings of the apostle Paul, also in the New Testament, and said they were also written under the inspiration of the Holy Spirit, calling his writings Scripture, just like the Old Testament.

> *And regard the patience of our Lord as salvation; just as also our beloved brother Paul, according to the wisdom given him, wrote to you, as also in all his letters, speaking in them of these things, in which are some things hard to understand, which the untaught and unstable distort, as they do also the rest of the Scriptures, to their own destruction.*

The Lord Jesus commissioned the apostles of the New Testament to teach in His name, with His authority. They were His apostles, which literally means, "One who is sent". This office can be compared to an ambassador sent by a ruler to speak for him. Jesus said in Luke 10:16,

> "The one who listens to you listens to Me, and the one who rejects you rejects Me; and he who rejects Me rejects Me rejects the One who sent Me."

To the writers of the New Testament, the Scriptures both Old and New Testaments were Scripture, the very breath of God, because the source, or origin of them, was God Himself. This is the same for the Lord Jesus as He commissioned the apostles with His authority. This is vital because no one can hold to the Old Testament without holding to the New Testament.

Jesus also taught that there is no way they could love the Father, love the God that the Jewish people thought they were honoring without loving and honoring Him as well. Rejection of Him is rejection of God the Father. Below is a sample of some of the verses where Jesus made this clear to the Jewish leaders who did not believe in Him.

> *"That all may honor the Son, just as they honor the Father. Whoever does not honor the Son does not honor the Father who sent Him."* (John 5:23)

> *"If I am not doing the works of My Father then do not believe Me; but if I do them, even though you do not believe Me, believe the works, that you may know and understand that the Father is in Me and I am in the Father."* (John 10:37-38)

> *"Which one of you convicts Me of sin? If I tell the truth, why do you not believe Me? Whoever is of God hears the Words of God. The Reason why you do not hear them is that you are not of God."* (John 8:46-47)

The New Testament is not just some work that a group is claiming should be put along with the sacred Scripture of the Old Testament. Both books are endorsed by the authority of none other than the Lord Jesus Christ Himself, and there is no contradiction found in the teaching between the two books. Why this all matters so much is that we are talking about Judaism in relation to Christianity, and there are people who would say that they embrace the Jewish faith but not Jesus; they say that the Messiah is definitely coming, and is predicted all throughout the Old Testament, but that he has not yet come. This is not possible in light of Jesus' teaching. First of all as we will see in the following chapter, no one could falsely fill all of the requirements of being the Messiah either by chance or design. God designed it that way. Jesus taught in the above passage and many others that it is not possible for people to love

God the Father and not love God the Son. People who renounce Jesus as Messiah are doing this, and if we truly love them, and care about their eternal destiny, we will want them to know the truth. We want to reflect the love of our Lord and pronounce what He taught. This is what He commanded us to do, to spread the message of the good news of salvation found in Jesus Christ our Lord. Jesus said to the Jewish leaders in John chapter 5:39,

> *"You search the Scriptures because you think that in them you have eternal life; it is these that testify about Me; and you are unwilling to come to Me so that you may have life."*

Jesus was telling them that they read and search through the Old Testament and in them they feel is the message of eternal life. They do this but then still reject Him. He was telling them that these same Scriptures that they were relying on for their eternal salvation were all about Him, they *"testified"* of Him. This whole book that I am writing here gets its cue from the Messiah who came for His people, people who searched the Scriptures in search of eternal life, when eternal life was standing right in front of them. That is why this book is designed the way that it is to show how you can't embrace Judaism without embracing the very one it all represents, and it is my heart's plea for all to see that.

Jesus goes on later in the same chapter, John 5:45,

> *"Do not think that I will accuse you before the Father; the one who accuses you is Moses, in whom you have set your hope. For if you believed Moses, you would believe Me, for he wrote about Me. But if you do not believe his writings, how will you believe My words?"*

Jesus purposely used Moses as a prime example to the Jewish people He was talking to. Jewish people will certainly tell you that they believe in Moses and what he taught. But as Jesus stated in the above passage, Moses was writing about Him, and if they truly believed in Moses they would believe in Him because as He said, He wrote of Him, and, as we have said the entire Old Testament writes of and points to Christ. He wrote of Him in Genesis chapter 3 (Genesis 3:15), as the seed of the woman who would come and destroy the works of the serpent. He wrote of Him in Deuteronomy 18 telling of a prophet who would come and speak the words of God and that He should be listened to.

> *"The Lord your God will raise up for you a prophet like me from among you, from your brothers-it is him you shall listen-I will raise up for them a prophet like you from their brothers. And I will put my words in his mouth. And he shall speak to them all I have commanded him. And whoever will not listen to my words that he shall speak in my name, I myself will require it of him.* (Deuteronomy 18:15, 18-19)

In Deuteronomy 34:10, this verse is interpreted of the coming Messiah, the ultimate prophet to come. The New Testament interprets this passage in the same way (Acts 3:22,23;7:37). Moses also wrote of Jesus in the story of the bronze serpent in Numbers 21:5-9. In Punishments of the people God sent serpents. The people could only be spared by looking up at the bronze snake Moses made and set it on top of a pole. This is one of many symbols of the Messiah to come and redeem the people. Jesus says in John 3:14,15:

> *"As Moses lifted up the serpent in the wilderness, even so must the Son of Man be lifted up; so that whoever believers will in Him have eternal life."*

Just as the snake had to be lifted up and the people look upon it for physical life, so must Jesus be lifted up so that all who believe on Him will have eternal, spiritual, life.

Jesus was making it clear that there is no way anyone can separate Him from belief in the Old Testament. He used the most cherished and foundational people from the Jewish faith to do so. He also told them that Abraham (the father of the Jewish people), rejoiced to see His day in John 8:58. It is not possible to claim to honor the God the Father, or love the God the Father, if one rejects the One whom He sent in the world to redeem the world. This was the thing that made me grieve over my own family's reaction, and also makes a strong statement about the need to evangelize all the Jewish people. These are a people who need Christ as much as anyone. We are privileged only through the grace of God to have received that and we need to share it with them. They have to know because they believe they are honoring God with their beliefs. True love for them would compel us to tell them and not worry about their reaction to us.

In the next chapter we elaborate on the Messiah-ship of Jesus, of how God put the clear identity of the Messiah all through the pages of the Old Testament so that His coming into the world would be unmistakable and indisputable.

6

The Messiah-ship of Jesus

> *"And he entered the synagogue and continued speaking out boldly for three months, reasoning and persuading them about the kingdom of God."* Acts 19:8

Many of the events and circumstances of the OT as we have said were symbols, shadows of what Messiah Jesus would do and accomplish for us. They all led up to the great coming of the Messiah.

John the Baptist, the herald, prophesied in the Old Testament, who would announce to the world the arrival of the Messiah, did so, right on cue. He shouted out for all to hear when the fullness of the moment arrived, "Repent, for the kingdom of heaven is at hand." John the Baptist came to the world as the herald for the Messiah. He would announce this greatest event in the history of mankind. John quotes from the prophet Isaiah:

> "THE VOICE OF ONE CRYING IN THE WILDERNESS, MAKE READY THE WAY OF THE LORD, MAKE HIS PATHS STRAIGHT. EVERY RAVINE WILL BE FILLED, AND EVERY MOUNTAIN AND HILL WILL BE BROUGHT LOW; THE CROOKED WILL BECOME STRAIGHT, AND THE ROUGH ROADS SMOOTH; AND ALL FLESH WILL SEE THE SALVATION OF GOD." (Luke 3:4-6 from Isaiah 40:3-5; and 52:10)

The moment every loyal Jew who loved God, longed for, had arrived. It was the breakthrough of the kingdom of God in this world, the glorious moment of their salvation!

The fulfillment of prophecy is the key. As we have said the Old Testament is filled with prophecies, predictions of future events that will take place because the Bible is the Word of God. This is also what makes the faith verifiable and objective. It deals with reality, with real historical events. This is not what many consider as faith. Many people are persuaded that the faith that they have is a leap in the dark as it were; believing with no reason to. Biblical faith as described in the book of Hebrews is by no means blind faith. Hebrews 11:1 says;

> *Now faith is the assurance of things hoped for, the conviction of things not seen.*

Biblical faith is assurance of the things God promises in His Word. It is complete assurance because of the character of God and what He has done. Since we know from what He has shown us, we can be assured of the future. (The word conviction, can also be translated *evidence*).

Peter tells us in 2 Peter 1:16, *for we did not follow cleverly devised tales when we made known to you the power and coming of our Lord Jesus Christ, but we were eyewitnesses of His majesty.*

Peter was setting himself and his teaching apart from the false teachers of his day who did conjure up tales, fables as they were, to draw disciples to themselves. He talked of being a witness, a direct observer of the events themselves. The events as recorded in Scripture are real and historical, and display the power and plans of God for His people. The prophecies of the coming Messiah are detailed and thorough. They could never be conjured up by anyone.

Shortly, we have a list of just some of the prophecies out of hundreds, of the Messiah who was to come. Prophecies which we see later in this chapter were recognized overwhelmingly by Jewish leaders hundreds of years before Jesus' day and hundreds of years after. This is key, because it is only recently in history that the rabbinical view on these passages has changed. Views that were held by rabbis for centuries have been altered, a curious development indeed. In the example of Isaiah chapter fifty three, a strong Messianic passage, which we will look at in greater detail, the Ashkenazi Jews eliminated it from their Bibles for centuries [3]. These prophecies were fulfilled perfectly by Jesus of Nazareth.

Mathematician Peter Stoner calculated the odds of someone fulfilling just eight of these prophecies by chance. It was one in ten to the seventeenth power. He compared those odds to filling the state of Texas completely with silver dollars two feet thick and marking out one, only one, and then being able to pick that one out, in one try [4]. Incredible indeed. There are almost three hundred total Messianic prophecies in the Old Testament. Here are just eighteen:[5] First the verse, or verses, that the prophecy was predicted in the Old Testament will be presented, then the verse in the New Testament where it was fulfilled:

1. <u>Messiah was to born in Bethlehem</u>; prophesied in Micah 5:2, fulfilled in Matthew 2:1-6; Luke 2:1-20.

Prophecy:

> *But as for you, Bethlehem Ephrathah, too little to be among the clans of Judah, from you One will come forth for Me to be ruler in Israel. His goings forth are from long ago, from the days of eternity.* (Micah 5:2)

Fulfillment:

> *Now after Jesus was born in Bethlehem of Judea in the days of Herod the king, magi from the east arrived in Jerusalem, saying, "Where is He who has been born King of the Jews? For we saw His star in the east and have come to worship Him." When Herod the king heard this, he was troubled, and all Jerusalem with him. Gathering together all the chief priests and scribes of the people, he inquired of them where*

---

[3] The Search for the Messiah, Mark Eastman, pg. 211
[4] Science speaks, Peter W. Stoner, pg. 109
[5] The Life Application Bible, pg. 1938

the Messiah was to be born? They said to him, "In Bethlehem of Judea; for this is what has been written by the prophet:
    'AND YOU, BETHLEHEM, LAND OF JUDAH, ARE BY NO MEANS LEAST AMONG THE LEADERS OF JUDAH; FOR OUT OF YOU SHALL COME FORTH A RULER WHO WILL SHEPHERD MY PEOPLE ISRAEL.'"
    (Matthew 2:1-6)

2. <u>Messiah was to be born of a virgin</u>; Isaiah 7:14; Matthew 1:18-25; Luke 1:26-38

    Prophecy:

    Therefore the Lord Himself will give you a sign: Behold, a virgin will be with child and bear a son, and she will call His name Immanuel. (Isaiah 7:14)

    Fulfillment:

    Now the birth of Jesus Christ was as follows: when His mother Mary had been betrothed to the Joseph, before they came together she was found to be with child by the Holy Spirit. And Joseph her husband, being a righteous man and not wanting to disgrace her, planned to send her away secretly. But when he had considered this, behold, and angel of the Lord. (Matthew 1:18-25)

3. <u>Messiah was to be a prophet like Moses</u>; Deuteronomy 18:15, 18, 19; John 7:40

    Prophecy:

    The Lord your God will raise up for you a prophet like Me from among you, from your countrymen, you shall listen to him.

I will raise up a prophet from among their countrymen like you, and I will put My words in his mouth, and he shall speak to them all that I command him.

It shall come about that whoever shall not listen to My words which he shall speak in My name, I Myself shall require it of him. (Deuteronomy 18:15, 18, 19)

Fulfillment:

Some of the people therefore, when they heard these words, were saying, "this certainly is the Prophet." (John 7:40)

4. <u>Messiah was to enter Jerusalem in triumph</u>; Zechariah 9:9; Matthew 21:1-9; John 12:12-16

Prophecy:

Rejoice greatly, O daughter of Zion! Shout in triumph, O daughter of Jerusalem! Behold your king is coming to you; He is just and endowed with salvation, humble and mounted on a donkey, even on a colt, the foal of a donkey. (Zechariah 9:9)

Fulfillment:

When they approached Jerusalem and had come to Bethpage, at the Mount of Olives, then Jesus sent two disciples, saying to them, "Go into the village opposite you, and immediately you will find a donkey tied there and a colt with her; unite them and bring them to Me. If anything says anything to you, you shall say, 'The Lord has need of them,' and immediately he will send them." This took place to fulfill what was spoken through the prophet:

"SAY TO THE DAUGHTER OF ZION,
BEHOLD YOUR KING S COMING TO

YOU, GENTLE, AND MOUNTED ON A DONKEY, EVEN ON A COLT, THE FOAL OF A BEAST OF BURDEN."'

The disciples went out and did just as Jesus had instructed them, and brought the donkey and the colt, and laid their coats on them; and He sat on the coats. Most of the crowd spread their coats on the road, and others were cutting branches from the trees and spreading them in the road. The crowds going ahead of Him, and those who followed, were shouting, "Hosanna to the Son of David; BLESSED IS HE WHO COMES IN THE NAME OF THE LORD; *Hosanna in the highest!"* (Matthew 21:1-9)

5. Messiah was to be rejected by His own people; Isaiah 53:1,3; Psalm 118:22; Isaiah 8:13-15; Matthew 26:3,4; John 12:17-43 (not listed below); Acts 4:1-12 (not listed below as well)

Prophecy:

Who has believed our message? And to whom has the arm of the Lord been revealed?

He was despised and forsaken of men, a man of sorrows and acquainted with grief; and like one from whom men hide their face He was despised, and we did not esteem Him. (Isaiah 53:1,3)

The stone which the builders rejected has become the chief cornerstone. (Psalm 118:22)

It is the Lord of hosts whom you should regard as holy. And He shall be your fear, and He shall be your dread. Then He shall become a sanctuary; but to both the houses of Israel, a stone to strike and a rock to stumble over, and a snare and a trap for the inhabitants of Jerusalem. Many will stumble over them, then they will fall and be broken; they will even be snared and caught. (Isaiah 8:13-15)

Fulfillment:

Then the chief priests and the elders of the people gathered together in the court of the high priest, named Caiaphas; and they plotted together to seize Jesus and killed Him. (Matthew 26:3,4)

6. <u>Messiah was to betrayed by one of His followers</u>; Psalm 41:9; Luke 22:19-23; Matthew 26:14-16, 47-50

Prophecy:

Even my close friend in whom I trusted, who ate my bread, has lifted up his heel against me. (Psalm 41:9)

Fulfillment:

And when He had taken some bread and given thanks, He broke it and gave it to them, saying, "This is My body which is given for you; do this is in remembrance of Me." And in the same way He took the cup after they had eaten, saying, "This cup which is poured out for you is the new covenant in My blood. But behold, the hand of the one betraying Me is with mine on the table. For indeed, the Son of Man is going as it has been determined; but woe to that man by whom He is betrayed!" And they began to discuss among themselves which one of them it might be who was going to do this thing. (Luke 22:19-23)

7. <u>Messiah was to be tried and condemned</u>; Isaiah 53:8; Matthew 27:1,2; Luke 23:1-25

   Prophecy:

   > *By oppression and judgment He was taken away; and as for His generation, who considered that He was cut off out of the land of the living for the transgression of my people, to whom the stroke was due? (Isaiah 53:8)*

   Fulfillment:

   > *Now when the morning came, all of the chief priests and the elders of the people conferred together against Jesus to put Him to death; and they bound Him, and led Him away and delivered Him to Pilate the governor. (Matthew 27:1,2)*

8. <u>Messiah was to be silent before His accusers</u>; Isaiah 53:7; Matthew 27:12-14; Mark 15:3-4; Luke 23:8-10

   Prophecy:

   > *He was oppressed and He was afflicted yet He did not open His mouth; like a lamb that is led to slaughter, and like a sheep that is silent before its shearers, so He did not open His mouth. (Isaiah 53:7)*

   Fulfillment:

   > *And while He was being accused by the chief priests and elders, He did not answer. Then Pilate said to Him, "Do you not hear how many things they testify against You?" And He did not answer him with regard to even a single charge, so the governor was quite amazed. (Matthew 27:12-14)*

9. <u>Messiah was to be struck and spat upon by His enemies</u>; Isaiah 50:6; Matthew 26:67; Matthew 27:30; Mark 14:65

Prophecy:

> *I gave My back to those who strike Me, and My cheeks to those who would pluck out the beard; I did not cover My face from humiliation and spitting.* (Isaiah 50:6)

Fulfillment:

> *Then they spat in His face and beat Him with their fists; and others slapped Him.* (Matthew 26:67)

10. <u>Messiah was to be mocked and insulted</u>; Psalm 22:7,8; Matthew 27:39-44; Luke 23:11, 35

Prophecy:

> *All who see me sneer at me; They separate with the lip, they wag the head, saying, "Commit yourself to the Lord; let Him deliver him; let Him rescue him, because He delights in him."* (Psalm 22:7,8)

Fulfillment:

> *And those passing by were hurling abuse at Him, wagging their heads and saying, "You who are going to destroy the temple and rebuild it in three days, save Yourself! If You are the Son of God, come down from the cross." In the same way the chief priests also, along with the scribes and elders, were mocking Him and saying, "He saved others; He cannot save Himself. He is the King of Israel; let Him now come down from the cross, and we will believe in Him. HE TRUSTS IN GOD; LET GOD RESCUE Him now, if HE DELIGHTS IN HIM; for He said, I*

am the Son of God." The robbers who had been crucified with Him were also insulting Him with the same words. (Matthew 27:39-44)

11. <u>Messiah was to die by crucifixion</u>; Psalm 22:14-17; Matthew 27:31; Mark 15:20,25

    Prophecy:

    I am poured out like water, and My bones are out of joint; my heart is like wax; it is melted within me. My strength is dried up like a potsherd, and my tongue cleaves to my jaws; and You lay me in the dust of death. For dogs have surrounded me; a band of evildoers has encompassed me; they pierced my hands and my feet. I can count all my bones. They look, they stare at me. (Psalm 22:14-17)

    Fulfillment:

    After they had mocked Him, they took the scarlet robe off Him and put His own garments back on Him, and led Him away to crucify Him. (Matthew 27:31)

12. <u>Messiah was to suffer with criminals and pray for His enemies</u>; Isaiah 53:12; Matthew 27:38; Mark 15:27; 28; Luke 23:32-34

    Prophecy:

    Therefore, I will allot Him a portion with the great, and He will divide the booty with the strong; because He poured out Himself to death, and was numbered with the transgressors; yet He Himself bore the sin of many, and interceded for the transgressors. (Isaiah 53:12)

Fulfillment:

At that time two robbers were crucified with Him, one on the right and one on the left. (Matthew 27:38)

But Jesus was saying, "Father, forgive them; for they do not know what they are doing." (Luke 23:32-34)

13. <u>Messiah was to be given vinegar and gall</u>; Psalm 69:21; Matthew 27:34; John 19:28-30

Prophecy:

They also gave me gall for my food and for my thirst they gave me vinegar to drink. (Psalm 69:21)

Fulfillment:

They gave Him wine to drink mixed with gall; and after tasting it, He was unwilling to drink. (Matthew 27:34)

14. <u>Others were to cast lots for Messiah's garments</u>; Psalm 22:18; Matthew 27:35; John 19:23, 24

Prophecy:

They divide my garments among them, and for my clothing they cast lots. (Psalm 22:18)

Fulfillment:

And when they had crucified Him, they divided up His garments among themselves by casting lots. (Matthew 27:35)

15. <u>Messiah's bones were not to be broken</u>; Exodus 12:46; Psalm 34:20; John 19:31-36

    Prophecy:

    > *It is to be eaten in a single house; you are not to bring forth any of the flesh outside of the house, nor are you to break any bone of it. (Exodus 12:46)*

    Prophecy:

    > *He keeps all his bones, not one of them is broken. (Psalm 34:20)*

    Fulfillment:

    > *Then the Jews, because it was the day of preparation, so that the bodies would not remain on the cross on the Sabbath (for that Sabbath was a high day), asked Pilate that their legs might be broken, and that they might be taken away. So the soldiers came, and broke the legs of the first man and of the other who was crucified with him; but coming to Jesus, when they saw that He was already dead, they did not break His legs. But one of the soldiers pierced His side with a spear, and immediately blood and water came out. And he who has seen has testified, and his testimony is true; and he knows that he is telling the truth, so that you also may believe. For these things came to pass to fulfill the Scripture, "NOT A BONE OF HIM SHALL BE BROKEN." (John 19:31-36)*

16. <u>Messiah was to die as a sacrifice for sin</u>; Isaiah 53:5, 6, 8, 10, 11, 12; John 1:29; 11:49-52; Acts 10:43; 13:38, 39

Prophecy:

But He was pierced through for our transgressions, He was crushed for our iniquities; the chastening for our well-being fell upon Him, and by His scourging we are healed.

All of us like sheep have gone astray, each of us has turned to his own way; but the Lord has caused the iniquity of us all to fall on Him.

By oppression and judgment He was taken away; and as for His generation, who considered that He was cut off out of the land of the living for the transgression of my people, to whom the stroke was due?

But the Lord was pleased to crush Him, putting Him to grief; if He would render Himself as a guilt offering, He will see His offspring, He will prolong His days, and the good pleasure of the Lord will prosper in His hand.

As a result of the anguish of His soul, He will see it and be satisfied; By His knowledge the Righteous One, My Servant, will justify the many, as He will bear their iniquities.

Therefore, I will allot Him a portion with the great, and He will divide the booty with the strong; because He poured out Himself to death, and was numbered with the transgressors; yet He Himself bore the sin of many, and interceded for the transgressors. (Isaiah 53:5, 6, 8, 10, 11, 12)

Fulfillment:

The next day he saw Jesus coming to him and said, "Behold, the Lamb of God who takes away the sin of the world." (John 1:29)

But one of them, Caiaphas, who was high priest that year, said to them, "You know nothing at all, nor do you take into account that it is expedient for you that one man die for the people, and that the whole nation not perish." Now he did not say this on his own initiative, but being high priest that year, he prophesied that Jesus was going to die for the nation, and not for the nation only, but in order that He might also gather together into one the children of God who are scattered abroad. (John 11:49-52)

Of Him all the prophets bear witness that through His name everyone who believes in Him receives forgiveness of sins. (Acts 10:43)

17. Messiah was to be raised from the dead; Psalm 16:10; Isaiah 53:8-12

Prophecy:

For You will not abandon my soul to Sheol; nor will you allow Your Holy One to undergo decay. (Psalm 16:10)

By oppression and judgment He was taken away; and as for His generation, who considered that He was cut off out of the land of the living for the transgression of my people, to whom the stroke was due?

But the Lord was pleased to crush Him, putting Him to grief; if He would render Himself as a guilt offering, He will see His offspring, He will prolong His days, and the good pleasure of the Lord will prosper in His hand.

As a result of the anguish of His soul, He will see it and be satisfied; By His knowledge the Righteous One, My Servant, will justify the many, as He will bear their iniquities.

Therefore, I will allot Him a portion with the great, and He will divide the booty with the strong; because He poured out Himself to death, and was numbered with the transgressors; yet He Himself bore the sin of many, and interceded for the transgressors. (Isaiah 53:8-12)

18. <u>Messiah is now at God's right hand</u>; Psalm 110:1; Mark 16:19; Luke 24:50, 51

Prophecy:

The Lord says to my Lord: "Sit at My right hand until I make Your enemies a footstool for Your feet." (Psalm 110:1)

Fulfillment:

So then, when the Lord Jesus had spoken to them, He was received up into heaven and sat down at the right hand of God.
And He led them as far as Bethany, and He lifted up His hands and blessed them. While He was blessing them, He parted from them and was carried up into heaven. (Mark 16:19)

These prophecies were based on the promise of God to send a Messiah to redeem the people. These prophecies of course are predicting future events. These events that are of the future are part of God's grand plan, the outworking of what is said in the book of Isaiah, the accomplishment of all His good pleasure. (Isaiah 46:10). We are so privileged to be a part of His plan and that this plan included salvation for His people. That salvation was promised in the Garden of Eden (Gen. 3:15), after Adam fell and consequently to all men as a result (Rom. 5:12), then continued throughout the Old Testament. Abraham heard the promise and how God would use him to be the father of His nation Israel (Gen. 15:6), and through them the whole world would be blessed (Gen. 22:18).

The Messiah, the Redeemer, would come through the Jews, He would be a Jew. There would be no mistaking it, this Messiah would be of the line of David, would be born in Bethlehem, would be born of a virgin, and the list goes on and on. These verses and these unmistakable attributes of this One to come were carefully studied by the Rabbis for centuries before He came into the world. We need to understand that the knowledge of the Old Testament and of the Hebrew language itself of the ancient rabbis far exceeds rabbis or more modern times and of our own. Even young teenage boys were required to memorize the Torah, the first books of the Old Testament. Rabbis were famous for memorization of large chunks of the Old Testament. This is important to remember when we look at the ancient rabbinical tradition, and their interpretations on Messianic passages of the Old Testament, passages that predicted of the future Messiah to come; interpretations that were made before the arrival of Jesus of Nazareth on the scene. The interpretations to the passages that are considered Messianic, speaking of the arrival of the Messiah to come, are in agreement as to how the ancient rabbis and Christians see them. It is interesting to note that any changes that occurred to the original understanding of what these texts were believed to be saying took many, many centuries.

We will look at some of these and see how the changes that were made by modern rabbis were more of a reaction to Christians and their presenting their faith than anything else.

These texts assure us of the future. Based on what God has done in the past we know that we can count on what God promises in the future, that is biblical faith, not a leap into the dark based on only a blind hope. The Bible tells as we saw earlier that we have assurance of things hoped for and conviction of things not seen. We have this based on what God has done. Hebrews 11:1 says,

> *Now faith is the assurance of things hoped for, the conviction* (or evidence) *of things not seen.*

So we know based on these passages telling of the coming of the Messiah, what is going to happen in redemptive history. We also have a portrait, an unmistakable one of the Messiah Himself. These detailed descriptions leave no doubt as to who the Messiah would be and to when He would arrive. It also does not allow any room for imposters. You can't fake the type of detailed and miraculous attributes of the Messiah's birth and life, it is not possible. This is why predictive prophecy is so important and why it is so powerful. In general, the predictive prophecies of the Bible are specific and so clear, so astounding, that they have led some critics to claim that certain books of the Bible were actually written later than the ones where the prophecies were fulfilled. Manuscript evidence and dating of these materials has shown this to be without merit.

(Books for further study on this subject include: The Text of the New Testament, Bruce Metzger; The Origin of the Bible, Philip Comfort; The New Testament Documents: Are They Reliable?, F.F. Bruce).

So the prophecies give us the unmistakable signature of God as to who His Messiah would be. It is interesting that the ones that are the most miraculous in nature and the most descriptive of Christ would come under the greatest attack. For example, most Christians have heard people scoff about the virgin birth. These prophecies are so crucial because this is how God will be glorified through the consummation of all that He promised. As well, this is how we will know the identity of the Messiah, be sure of His authenticity.

Some will reject any of the miraculous events of the Bible regardless of what they are, their rejection is immediate and prior to any investigation. Their instantaneous rejection is based then on a naturalistic bias, that is, anything that smacks of the supernatural is dismissed immediately without discussion. We are then labeled as unsophisticated and from a time period that they say is long gone. But truth is never outdated, it never goes out of style. To not even look at the evidence is simply being obscurantist, sticking one's head in the sand as it were. The Bible has shown itself to be a book with supernatural origins, from its detailed predictive prophecies, and amazing internal consistency. You have 66 books, written by over forty authors, over a time period of some 1600 years, from varied settings such as battlefields, royal palaces, the most remote corners of the desert, yet keeping a clear and unparalleled flow of the theme and teachings. There is manuscript evidence, or copies, with no rival for any ancient document, which actually includes an unheard of number of copies for historical study, and agreement among the copies. In addition, the time between the writings of the copies we have and the originals is incredibly early.

In his book, The Case for Christ, author Lee Strobel interviewed many of the world's leading experts pertaining to evidence for the Bible. One of the scholars that he interviewed was Bruce Metzger, a man who's reputation precedes him. During the interview Strobel asked how the Bible stacks up in comparison to other ancient documents. Documents to which history professors do not have any qualms in quoting as reliable. Such documents are confidently sited and not criticized. The Bible, however is not given such consideration, it falls into a completely different level of criticism. But seeing the reality of the documents we do have, the copies, manuscripts of the Old and New Testaments, it paints a very different picture. Strobel writes:

"When you talk about a great multiplicity of manuscripts," I said, "how does that contrast with other ancient books that are routinely accepted by scholars as reliable? For instance, tell me about the writing of authors from about the time of Jesus,"

Having anticipated the question, Metzger referred to some hand-written notes he had brought along.

"Consider Tacitus, the Roman historian who wrote his *Annals of Imperial Rome* in about A.D. 116," he began. "His first six books exist today in only one manuscript, and it was copied about A.D. 850. Books eleven through sixteen are in another manuscript dating from the eleventh century. Books seven through ten are lost. So there is a long gap between the time that Tacitus sought his information and wrote it down and the only existing copies."[6]

Strobel then asked how many copies of the New Testament do we have currently?

Metzger's eyes got wide. "More than five thousand have been cataloged," he said with enthusiasm, his voice going up an octave." That was a mountain of manuscripts compared to the anthills of Tacitus and Josephus! "Is that unusual in the ancient world? What would the runner-up be?" I asked.

"The quantity of New Testament material is almost embarrassing in comparison with other works of antiquity," he said. "Next to the New Testament, the greatest amount of manuscript testimony is of Homer's *Iliad*, which was the Bible of the ancient Greeks. There are some fewer

---

[6] The Case for Christ, Lee Strobel, pgs. 60-61

than 650 Greek manuscripts of it today. Some are quite fragmentary. They come down to us from the second and third century A.D. and following. When you consider that Homer composed his epic about 800 B.C., you can see there's a very lengthy gap."

"Very lengthy" was an understatement; it was a thousand years!

The agreement between these documents is astounding as well. Biblical scholars Geisler and Nix have concluded: "The New Testament, then, has not only survived in more manuscripts than any other book from antiquity, but it has survived in a purer form than any other book-a form that is 99.5 percent pure."[7]

But in terms of the prophecies of Jesus as the Messiah and perhaps of all of the miracles associated with Jesus, the virgin birth engenders the most controversy. There have been critics that have claimed that the word for virgin in the text, in Hebrew, *Almah*, in Greek *parthenos*, could be translated as young woman. As a side note, the Old Testament was written in Hebrew, and the New Testament in Greek. Around the year 250 B.C., a group of seventy rabbis translated the Old Testament into Greek, as this was the common language of the time and many Jewish people could not, or were not, reading Hebrew anymore. They translated the Hebrew *Almah*, into the Greek word *Parthenos*, meaning virgin. This is significant because as we have said earlier, they had a much better command of the Hebrew language than modern rabbis do and they lived much closer to the time when the originals were written.

The modern changes to the usage of the word virgin to young woman is much more likely a reaction to the claim of Christians as Jesus as Messiah than sincere scholarship. An example is found in the writings of Shlomo Yizchaki, better known as Rashi (1040-1105)[8]. He claimed that in this passage the *Almah* means young woman and not a virgin. He also was the first to claim that in Isaiah 53 the suffering servant was Israel and not the Messiah, which we discuss later in this chapter.

Arnold Fruchtenbuam, in his book, *Jesus was a Jew*, discusses Rashi's point of view and its' inconsistency with the rest of his interpretations using the word *Alma*:

---

[7] A General Introduction to the Bible, Geisler, Nix, page 367
[8] Jesus was Jew, Arnold Fruchtenbaum, Pg. 35

"Often Rashi is the one quoted as showing that ALMAH means "young woman." It is true that Rashi interpreted Isaiah 7:14 to mean a young woman, perhaps for the same reason he made Isaiah 53 refer to Israel and not the Messiah. But this is not enough to prove that Rashi always made ALMAH to mean a young woman. This Hebrew word is also found in the Song of Solomon 1:3 and 6:8. In these passages Rashi makes ALMAH to mean "virgin"! So, regardless of how Rashi interpreted Isaiah 7:14, he elsewhere did use the word ALMAH to mean "virgin." Furthermore, Rashi admitted that many Jewish scholars of his day made Isaiah 7:14 refer to a virgin. It can easily be seen that Rashi was trying to counteract Christian polemics with his interpretation of Isaiah 7:14 rather than being honest with the text itself. Also, as in the case of Isaiah 53, Rashi was again going contrary to popular Jewish interpretation."

It is true, that a secondary meaning for this word can be "young woman." The first thing that we must remember when approaching any Scripture, or any writing, is to look at the context it is written in. We saw in terms of the original prophecy in Isaiah it spoke of God providing "a sign," something extraordinary about this birth that was to take place. In this context the passage speaks so clearly that we really don't need to go beyond it. We read of the visitation to Mary of the angel Gabriel who told her of God's plan for her to conceive a Son who she shall name Jesus.

Mary answers saying, "How can this be, since I am a virgin?" Mary was amazed at this announcement because she had never been with a man as she said. This is why to her it was not possible.

She was young but in her culture she was certainly not too young to be a mother of children. But her reaction would make sense if she was indeed a virgin. This episode in the New Testament is the fulfillment of an Old Testament prophecy of the Messiah's birth in the book of Isaiah, chapter 7, verse 14 (Isaiah 7:14). The rabbis of the times since Isaiah have seen this passage as referring to the coming Messiah and that His birth would be extraordinary.

> *Therefore the Lord himself will give you a sign: Behold, a virgin with be with child and bear a son, and she will call His name Immanuel.*

Here we see the underlying prophecy behind the virgin birth. It is said that the Lord will give a sign. This means that God is going to do something special, something out of the ordinary, perhaps miraculous. These signs are used by God to point us to something far greater. We see again the importance of relying on the context of the passage to guide us to what is being said. In this case it is the significance, which comes from the word sign, of what God Himself is going to do. It says that the Lord will give a sign through the birth of this child. There will be something of godly significance in this event. God's prophet, His inspired spokesman Isaiah tells us that a virgin will be with child and will bear a son. This is why Mary said it <u>cannot</u> be, for the same reason that the miraculous nature of the prophecy in Isaiah tells us it will be a sign from God. A woman who is a virgin giving birth to a child would be miraculous, and certainly perceived as a sign from God.

A woman and her husband of five years going into a hospital to have a baby, is certainly nothing that doesn't happen every day all over the world. It is without a doubt an amazing thing how God designed us, and how the baby is formed, and grows in the mother to full term. All of this is nothing short of incredible. But it is not a miracle, not in the biblical sense. In the Bible a miracle, written in the original languages as either signs, wonders, or powers, the word miracle not being used, but it is something God does that is contrary to nature. Something that happens every day, all over the place, as extraordinary as it is, is not a miracle. But a virgin birth, now that is a miracle. If it is a normal birth how could it be seen as a sign?

It has been asserted by some that the New Testament writers simply misinterpreted the prophecy in the passage. This creates insurmountable problems for people who hold this view and profess to be Christians. 2 Peter 1:21 says that the men who wrote the Bible did not come up with this by their own initiative but they spoke from God as they were led by the Holy Spirit. Its origin was God. We are told that they were led by the Holy Spirit, the Spirit of truth (John 14:17). Did the Spirit of truth, God Himself (Acts 5:3-4), lead the apostles into error? Jesus told the apostles that the Spirit would lead them to all truth (John 16:13) God would certainly not lead anyone into error. In addition to this, the ancient rabbis interpreted this text in that way as the writers of the New Testament did.

Another major Messianic prophecy that we need to mention is Isaiah fifty three. This chapter presents the description of the Messiah and His work so clearly that as we mentioned earlier in the chapter some Jewish groups have left it out all together. Before going into the specifics of it and how the ancient rabbis interpreted it, we need to just read it. When a person hears the whole passage they can't help be struck with the clarity of the message, they know who it is talking about. It is an amazing description of the life of Jesus of Nazareth. I am Jewish and I remember before becoming a Christian, my reaction to hearing this passage. I thought about how much that sounded like Jesus of Nazareth.

For a person to be seen as embodying any prophecy in the Bible they would have to fulfill the prophecy perfectly. After listening to the one's we mention here, go further, delve into further study of this topic and see what you find. The books that I have referenced in this book could serve as helpful tools to help someone go further in their investigation of this most crucial of topics for anyone's life. But read this passage and see what message the Word of God is conveying here. Isaiah 52:13-15 and Isaiah 53:1-12:

> *Behold, My servant will prosper, He will high and lifted up and greatly exalted. Just as many were astonished at you, My people, so His appearance was marred more than any man and His form more than the sons of men. Thus He will sprinkle many nations, kings will shut their mouths on account of Him; for what had not been told them they will see, and what they had not heard they will understand.*
>
> *Who has believed our message? And to whom has the arm of the Lord been revealed? For He grew up before Him like a tender shoot, and like a root out of parched ground; He had no stately form or majesty that we should look upon Him, nor appearance that we should be attracted to Him. He was despised and forsaken of men, a man of sorrows and acquainted with grief; and like one from whom men hide their face He was despised, and we did not esteem Him.*

> *Surely our griefs He Himself bore, and our sorrows He carried; yet we ourselves esteemed Him stricken, smitten of God and afflicted. But He was pierced through for our transgressions, He was crushed for our iniquities; the chastening for our well-being fell upon Him, and by His scourging we are healed. All of us like sheep have gone astray, each of us has turned to his own way; but the Lord has caused the iniquity of us all to fall on Him.*
>
> *He was oppressed and He was afflicted, yet He did not open His mouth; like a lamb led to slaughter, and like a sheep that is silent before its shearers, so He did open His mouth. By oppression and judgment He was taken away; and as for His generation, who considered that He was cut off out of the land of the living for the transgression of my people, to whom the stroke was due?*
>
> *His grave was assigned with wicked men, yet He was with a rich man in His death, because He had done no violence, nor was there any deceit in His mouth.*
>
> *But the Lord was pleased to crush Him, putting Him to grief; if He would render Himself as a guilt offering, He will see His offspring, He will prolong His days, and the good pleasure of the Lord will prosper in His hand. As the result of the anguish of His soul, He will see it and be satisfied; by His knowledge the Righteous One, My Servant, will justify the many, as He will bear their iniquities. Therefore, I will allot Him a portion with the great, and He will divide the booty with the strong; because He poured out Himself to death, and He was numbered with the transgressors; Yet He Himself bore the sin of many, and He interceded for the transgressors.*

It is easy to see from one read of this passage why it causes such a stir. It is a description of the person and work, and especially the work of Jesus Messiah.

I remember reading this to someone and when I was done they looked at me and said, "That sounds exactly like Jesus of Nazareth!"

They couldn't believe how clearly it described Him. This was someone who was not familiar with the Scriptures, had not heard it before and was just reacting solely to the weight of the description.

This prophecy in Isaiah fifty three explains much about what the Messiah to come would be like and what would be the nature of His mission here. It tells starting in verse one and going through three, of how His own people would reject Him and this explains the reaction of the Jewish people to His coming. People have asked me, "Well, if He is the Messiah, why have so many Jewish people rejected Him?" The Scriptures tell us that He would be rejected and that was one of the prophecy that the genuine Messiah would have to fulfill. The prophecy goes so far to tell us that He would also be despised, not esteemed by the people. He was not accused Jesus of sin, or were His miracles denied, the source was refuted. They saw the miracles firsthand and could not deny them. They were saying that Jesus' power was from the devil:

> *The Jews answered Him, "Are we not right in saying that you are a Samaritan and have a demon?" Jesus answered, "I do not have a demon, but I honor My Father, and you dishonor Me. Yet I do not seek My own glory; there is One who seeks it, and He is the judge. Truly, truly, I say to you, if anyone keeps My Word, he will never see death." (John 8:48-51)*

This chapter in Isaiah fifty three describes starting in verse four in vivid detail the all important Messianic prophecy of the substitutionary atonement that He would present for His people (Isaiah 53:4). Here is our salvation. Our substitute has come. He will take our place and pay for all of our sins against God.

We have been granted a substitute. It is the only way. It was told how the Messiah would come and suffer all of the punishments for all of God's people. He would be smitten of God and afflicted, be pierced through for our transgressions, crushed for our iniquities, our sin. But the promise 700 years before the Messiah came was that by His scourging we would be healed. The result of His atoning sacrifice, the result of His taking our place in facing the judgment of God is that we would be healed, we would be saved, made right with God. This is why this prophecy is so astonishing and so revealing.

This whole story of redemption is certainly nothing new. It is not a Christian invention. This story of redemption is woven throughout the whole Bible, start to finish. All that is part of belief in Jesus as Messiah is in the Old Testament, and is interpreted that way. Now if the ancient rabbis before the Messiah came did not see all of the Messianic prophecies that way someone might be able to make that case and cry foul. The truth of the matter is that they did view the Messianic prophecies in accordance with the view that believers in the Messiah, Christians, Jesus did in the first century and today. There is ample evidence available to us as we have the ancient writings of the rabbis to read and study.

There is more in Isaiah fifty three. We saw how the Messiah would not fight His treatment, would not open His mouth in defense, that He would be killed, and as in verse eight re-elaborates, *"for the transgression of my people, to whom the stroke was due?"* Again, the substitution atoning death of the Messiah is told of here. He took upon Himself what we had earned, what was due us, this is the gospel, the good news that is preached throughout the land. He voluntarily came down to our low estate and sacrificed Himself willingly. Jesus said in John chapter ten,

> *"I am the good shepherd; the good shepherd lays down His life for the sheep."* (John 10:11)

> *"For this reason the Father loves Me, because I lay down My life so that I may take it again."* (John 10:17)

> *"No one has taken it away from Me, but I lay it down on My own initiative, I have authority to lay it down, and I have authority to take it up again."* (John 10:18)

The sacrifice of the Messiah at the cross was voluntary on His part and necessary because we are completely unable to help ourselves in regard to our position with God. So God left glory for a time, fully God and fully man, to come here and take our place and make a way back to God for us. It was the greatest act of love, humility, and mercy that the world has ever and will ever witness. This is described for us in Philippians 2:5-8,

> *Have this attitude in yourselves which was also in Christ Jesus, who, although existing in the form of God, did not regard equality with God a thing to be grasped, but emptied Himself, taking the form of a bond-servant, and being made in the likeness of men. Being found in appearance as a man, He humbled Himself by becoming obedient to the point of death, even death on a cross.*

The description continues by telling how he would die with criminals and be assigned a criminal's death, but that He was with a rich man in His death. In the burial accounts of the gospels, Joseph of Arimathea, a member of the Jewish ruling body, the Sanhedrin, a very rich man indeed, requested Jesus' body from Pontius Pilate and prepared for burial and placed it in his family tomb (John 19:38).

That the Messiah would be without sin is seen, and something that is expected of the Messiah, not new addition, but we are told that in verse nine of chapter fifty three in Isaiah that, *"He had done no violence, nor was there any deceit in His mouth."* (Isaiah 53:9)

This is all part of the perfect flow of Old Testament prophecy into the New, and the perfect fulfillment of Jesus with all of the prophecies preceding Him. No one was able to convict Him of sin. Jesus asked in John 8,

"Which one of you convicts Me of sin?" No one was ever able to do so. (John 8:46)

In verse ten of Isaiah fifty three it says how the Lord was pleased to crush Him, putting Himself to grief if He would offer Himself as a *guilt offering* or *atonement for sin* (Isaiah 53:10). It pleased the Lord as it was part of His sovereign plan in which to redeem His people. This was part of His sovereign plan before the world was, a merciful plan that the through the righteousness of the Messiah, which we can attain through faith in Him, we would be holy and blameless before Him. Because of the righteousness of Christ applied to us who believe, we would be seen as righteous in God's eyes, therefore able to be in fellowship with Him in heaven. The Book of Ephesians describes this in chapter one:

> *...just as He chose us in Him before the foundation of the world, that we would be holy and blameless before Him.*
>
> *In love He predestined us to adoption as sons through Christ Jesus to Himself, according to the kind intention of His will,*
>
> *To the praise of the glory of His grace, which He freely bestowed upon us in the Beloved.*
>
> *In Him we have redemption through His blood, the forgiveness of our trespasses, according to the riches of His grace.* (Ephesians 1:4-7)

The Messiah that was to come as promised by God to the Jewish people would be offered as a perfect sacrifice for the sins committed against God by the people. This is the same message of good news, or the gospel that Christians profess. Its' roots are in the Old Testament prophecies of the coming Messiah. This is exactly what God said the Messiah would do. The people knew that they did not keep the Law of God perfectly, and that anyone who did not keep it was under a curse.

> *"Cursed is anyone who does not confirm the words of this law by doing them."* (Deut. 27:26).

Whoever does not keep the Law perfectly is under the judgment and condemnation of God. The Jewish people knew and understood this. This is affirmed, quoted in the New Testament book of Galatians, chapter three, verse ten. One violation of the Law brings this upon a person as seen in Deuteronomy chapters 27 and 28.

For example, in verse 1 of chapter 28:

> *"Now it shall be, if you diligently obey the Lord your God, being careful to do all His commandments which I command you today, the Lord your God will set you high above all the nations of the earth."* (Deuteronomy 28:1)

This is also reiterated in the book of James of the New Testament, chapter two, verse ten.

> *For whoever keeps the whole law and yet stumbles at one point, he has become guilty of all.* (James 2:10)

But thanks to God, He decreed that someone would keep the whole law, every point, and that would be applied to us who believe and trust in that. As verse nine said in Isaiah fifty three, He had done no violence or was any deceit in His mouth. (Isaiah 53:9) He was, without sin.

As well, this same one would take all of our punishment which was earned and is deserved upon Himself. This is the story of our redemption and the story of the Isaiah chapter fifty three. He was a guilt offering, offered for our sin. As it says further in verse eleven, He would, the Righteous One, justify the many, as He would bare their iniquities (Isaiah 53:11). Those who believe in Him would be declared just before God because the Messiah bore their sins, He took on their punishment for them, and gives His perfect righteousness to them, puts to their account. They now have His goodness applied to them, and have their sins paid for and can now have fellowship with God forever in heaven. Verse twelve says it again, *"he would bare the sin of many."* (Isaiah 53:12)

Again, this is all part of the natural flow from the Old to the New Testament. We see over and over again, and will never see otherwise, that there is a perfect movement from prophecy (Old Testament), to fulfillment, (New Testament).

We see finally in verse eleven that *"as a result of His aguish He will it and be satisfied"* (Isaiah 53:11), and in verse twelve that *"He be allotted a portion with the great, and divide the booty with the strong"* (Isaiah 53:12). The death of the Messiah would not be final, He would be resurrected. Psalm 16:10 (seen as a Messianic prophecy), says;

> *"For You will not abandon my soul to Sheol; nor will You allow Your Holy One to undergo decay."*

It is important to show at this point how the ancient rabbis interpreted this verse. Now we have to remember that these men were not followers of Jesus but rabbis of the Jewish faith who following the basic tenant of that faith, were looking for the coming Messiah. They wrote what they took these verses to mean.

In Mark Eastman's book, *The Search for the Messiah*, He covers in a detailed manner the many interpretations of the rabbis toward clearly Messianic prophecies. He proves that the interpretations of the rabbis match the Christian understanding of these passages. It was only much later that these passages were changed to counter the Christian view of the Messiah.

From the time of the development of the written Talmud (200-500 C.E.) this portion of Scripture was believed to be Messianic. In fact, it was not until the eleventh century C.E. that it was seriously proposed otherwise. At this time a rabbi named Shlomo Yizchaki, better known as Rashi (c. 1040-1105), began to interpret the suffering servant in these passages as reference to the nation of Israel. One of the oldest translations of the Hebrew Scriptures is known as the Targums. These are Aramaic translations of very ancient Hebrew manuscripts that also included commentary on the Scriptures. They were translated in the first or second century B.C.E. in the Targum of Isaiah, where we read this incredible quote regarding the suffering in Isaiah 53:

> "Behold, My Servant the Messiah shall proper; he shall be exalted and great and very powerful. The Righteous One shall grow up before him, lo, like sprouting plants; and like a tree sends its roots by the water-courses, so shall the exploits of the holy one multiply in the land which was desperate for him. His appearance shall not be a profane appearance, nor shall the awe of an ignorant person, but his countenance shall radiate with holiness, so that all who see him shall become wise through him. All of us were scattered like sheep…but it is the will of God to pardon the sins of all of us on his account… Then I will apportion unto him the spoil of great nations…because he was ready to suffer martyrdom that the rebellious he might subjugate to the Torah. And he might seek pardon for the sins of many."[9]

---

[9] The Search for the Messiah, Mark Eastman, pg. 18

As was mentioned in the above quote it was a very late invention but some have attempted to make the suffering servant in this verse be the nation of Israel instead of the Messiah. The late date of these objections makes the entire change in interpretation very suspect, but the problems with this are numerous. First of all this would be going against the body of writings that ancient rabbis have held to for centuries regarding this passage being understood as pointing to the Messiah. So they would be going against their own tradition, that of their own rabbis, to attempt to prove this point. At the time this was written, there was objection from among their own people, some among the most distinguished rabbis of their time.[10]

The lengthy passage of Isaiah fifty three is riddled with personal pronouns such as He, Him, His, as opposed to the use of We, Us, and Our, we has to referring to the prophet Isaiah who wrote this prophecy and the nation of Israel who are his people that he is speaking of. Until Rashi, all Jewish theology taught that this referred to the Messiah. Since Rashi, most of rabbinical theology has taught that it refers to Israel.[11]

Fruchtenbaum points out that there are several problems with the interpretation of the Suffering servant being Israel.[12] The first was mentioned above. Next is how the Suffering Servant dies (verse 8), and that death as Isaiah said, is "for my people" who are Isaiah's people? We know that Isaiah's people are the nation of Israel. If "my people' refers to Israel they can't also be the Suffering Servant. The Suffering Servant is presented as innocent (verses 4-6, 8*b*, 9*b*).

The Jewish people were never portrayed in the Bible as innocent, and the people were punished many times as a result. Other problems include how the Suffering Servant was portrayed as voluntary, as silent and opening His mouth under this affliction. This again is not certainly the case as seen in Scripture where the Jewish people cry out to God in affliction. In verses 4-6, 8, 10, 12, the death of the Suffering Servant is seen as for others as a substitution for others and so they would not have to suffer for their sins (Isaiah 53:4-6, 8, 10, 12). There is no where in

---

[10] Jesus was Jew, Arnold Fruchtenbaum, pgs.30-35
[11] ibid., pg. 42
[12] ibid., pg. 44-46

Scripture that the Jewish people ever died for the Gentiles or non-Jews and Israel indeed suffered in the Scriptures but it was for their own sins.

Fruchtenbaum shows how the sufferings here bring justification and spiritual healing to all those who accept it, that this sacrifice would result in death for the Servant, and most importantly that this death would not be final but that He would be resurrected.7. There is no reason to break from any of the traditional understandings of these verses, and any other explanation such as the Suffering Servant being the nation of Israel, is not plausible.

There are other examples of agreement in ancient Jewish writings such as the Talmud that agree with a Christian understanding of these verses pointing to the Messiah. These are commentaries from the ancient rabbis as to what this verse meant.

"This teaches us that *God will burden the Messiah* with commandments and sufferings as with millstones."[13]

> "There is a whole discussion in the Talmud about the Messiah's name. The several discussants suggested various names and cited several Scriptural references in support of these names. The disciples of the school of Rabbi Yehuda Ha' Nasi said, 'The sick one is his name,' for as it written, *'Surely he has borne our sickness and carried our sorrows and pains, yet we considered him stricken, smitten, and afflicted of God.'*"[14]

Psalm twenty two is another of hundreds of Messianic prophecies of the Messiah. It is also another such as Isaiah fifty three that when read bares a startling resemblance to Jesus of Nazareth, as it should, it was written about Him so we would recognize Him, so it would be unmistakable, and could not be imitated.

The following is verses 1-18.

---

[13] Talmud, Sanhedrin 93b, from The Search for the Messiah, Mark Eastman, pg. 20

[14] ibid., pg.20

My God, my God, why have You forsaken me? Far from my deliverance are the words of my groaning. O my God, I cry by day, but You did not answer; and by night, but I have no rest. Yet You are holy. O You who are enthroned upon the praises of Israel. In You our fathers trusted; they trusted and You delivered them. To You they cried out and were delivered; in You they trusted and were not disappointed.

But I am a worm and not a man, a reproach of men and despised by the people. All who see me sneer at me; they separate with the lip, they wag the head saying, "Commit yourself to the Lord; let Him deliver him; let Him rescue him, because He delights in Him."

Yet You are He who brought Me forth from the womb; You made me trust upon my mother's breasts. Upon You I was cast from birth; You have been my God from my mother's womb.

Be not far from me, for trouble in near; for there is none to help. Many bulls have surrounded me; strong bulls of Bashan have encircled me. They open wide their mouth at me, as a ravening and a roaring lion. I am poured out like water, and all my bones are out of joint; my heart is like wax; it is melted within me. My strength is dried up like a potshard, and my tongue cleaves to my jaws; and You lay me in the dust of death. For dogs have surrounded me; a band of evildoers has encompassed me; they pierced my hands and my feet. I can count all my bones. They look, they stare at me; they divide my garments among them, and for my clothing they cast lots. (Psalm 22:1-18)

This was the Psalm Jesus quoted on the cross. It is unmistakably Messianic. Within this Psalm is a description of the sufferings of the Messiah, these are unmistakably about the crucifixion of Christ. The descriptions remarkably fit (but with all of God's plans, it is expected for the outcome to happen as promised) the suffering that Jesus endured on the cross. The description of death by crucifixion is what is so striking. He is poured out like water, his bones are out of joint, his heart is like wax, his strength is dried up like a potshard, and his tongue cleaves to his jaws. Think of someone on a cross, thirsty, having no more strength left due to the magnitude of the stress. When you are hung on a cross in crucifixion, long spikes driven through your wrists and feet, you have to lift yourself up to breathe. As you run out of strength to do so you begin to suffocate.

Your bones would be put out of joint as they stretched you to fit on the cross, and then hung by them, supporting all of your weight. This would certainly strain the joints beyond what they could bear. *"They pierced my hands and feet."* David, under the inspiration of the Holy Spirit, describes this method of execution centuries before it was ever invented. We have physical evidence as well that the hands and the feet of the victims were indeed pierced as the gospels describe.[15] In Matthew 27:35 and John 19:23, 24 we see the prophecy fulfilled by the guards who cast lots for the clothing of Jesus.

There are so many more examples that could be given but it is beyond the scope of this book. The detail of the prophecies and the exact fulfillment of them by Jesus of Nazareth left no doubt as to who He was. The Messiah arrived right on schedule, and came first for His people, the Jewish people.

In Luke chapter two we meet a man who was given a very special gift from God. He was told that he would not die until he saw the Messiah, the Savior. His name was Simeon. Every day faithful Simeon waited and watched in the temple for the King to come.

As he knew any promise of God would have to come true, he never wavered. He must have endured a great deal of mockery upon being asked why he is at the temple every day watching diligently. It makes one immediately think of faithful Noah, obeying God, and waiting on His faithfulness, building the ark, enduring scorn and ridicule until the flood came.

Then one day Mary and Joseph entered the temple holding their baby. Simeon held the baby after the ceremony and looked toward heaven and sang a great song of praise to God and to the keeping of His promise.

---

[15] The Case for Christ, Lee Strobel, pgs. 200-201

> *...and when the parents brought in the child Jesus, to carry out for Him the custom of the Law, then he took Him into his arms, and blessed God and said,*
>
> *"Now Lord, You are releasing Your bond-servant to depart in peace, according to Your word; for my eyes have seen Your salvation, which You have prepared in the presence of all peoples, A LIGHT OF REVELATION TO THE GENTILES, and the glory of Your people Israel"* (Luke 2:27-32)

The child grew and became a man. All of the predictions of God were fulfilled in Him. All of the promises of God up to this point brought to fruition.

After the great act of redemption of the cross the Bible describes at the end of the Book of Luke an amazing event that occurred as two men walked despondently away from Jerusalem and lamented at what they had just seen. They had seen their Lord crucified, they thought it was over. They did not understand, they thought that all of their hopes were dashed and their Messiah had not arrived. The next verse comes to my mind often when I'm witnessing to my Jewish brothers and sisters. It is all from Luke chapter twenty four. These same two men then meet a man along the way as they walk not realizing his true identity. The man walking and talking with them on the road is Jesus Himself. He asked them what they were talking about. They tell Jesus in shock how could he not know what just happened and what they are discussing. Jesus asked them what happened (of course knowing full well what just occurred). They then explain how their teacher and leader was killed, and how they had hoped that he was going to redeem Israel. With the two men still unaware of who was telling them, Jesus then explained all that I have been trying to teach in this book in one perfect lesson. He summed it all up when he told them,

> *"O foolish men and slow of heart to believe in all that the prophets have spoken! Was it not necessary for the Christ to suffer these things and to enter into His glory?*

Then beginning with Moses and with all the prophets, He explained to them the things concerning Himself in all the Scriptures." (Luke 24:25)

He explained to them that all that the prophets wrote in the Old Testament was true and was about Him. It all led up to this moment just as God had planned it to. Jesus described people as foolish and slow of heart who would not believe this obvious connection. This is what the Old Testament is about, the things concerning the Christ who was to come and has now come, and has surely entered into His glory!

7

My Burden For My People

I remember the effect on me after reading about the conversion of the apostle Paul, perhaps the most passionate follower of the Lord Jesus, in the New Testament, and of his amazing Spirit-powered work of evangelism for the rest of his life. What struck me so personally was his passionate burden for his people to know God. He was a Jew as I am. Upon reading his feelings toward his people I was brought into touch with the overwhelming feelings that I have upon discussions of God with them. When one of my people would reject Christ and His Messiah-ship, I felt such a deep sadness, one that cut deeper than any experience of witnessing to someone. You feel the heartbreak in the way the apostle described his laments for his people upon their rejection of the message he brought to them. As a fellow Jew I know so well and can relate to these feelings. This all must have been especially tough for Paul because he was the most outstanding of Jews. He was, as he described himself, the Jew of Jews.

The apostle was taught by Gamaliel, a student of the rabbi Hillel, who is perhaps the most famous rabbi who has ever lived. Paul, called Saul at the time, was a Pharisee, a sect of the Jews, which was the most strident and meticulous in their keeping of the Jewish traditions. Saul, was especially zealous even for them, to say the least. Before his recognition of the Messiah, he had requested papers to go out in search of followers of Jesus, people called, interestingly enough, "The people of the Way." He was going out no matter what the hardship, no matter how long he had to travel in the arid desert, to track them down. He wanted to search for them to wipe out what he thought was a heretical affront to Judaism. His goal being to bring them in for trial and imprisonment.

He did in fact obtain permission from his superiors to do this and headed out on his journey down the Damascus road. His journey was suddenly and astonishingly interrupted one day when he was struck by a brilliant light from heaven which blinded him and knocked him to the ground. He then heard the voice of the Lord Jesus asking him why he was persecuting Him? (Acts 22:7), (To God, an assault on His church was an assault on Him). Saul answered, "Who are you Lord?" (Acts 22:8) The voice answered him saying that he was Jesus, whom he was persecuting. (Acts 22:8) He then had him rise and go into the city to see a man whom God appointed to help Saul begin his new work for God. His life was changed forever in that astonishing instant. He had seen "the light" as no one else ever had. The Holy Spirit opened his eyes and changed Saul's heart as He does with all believers and sent him on the greatest missionary journey the world has ever seen. His life was from then on dedicated to telling people of the Messiah who had indeed come and even appeared to him.

The apostle described this amazing experience of his conversion in The Book of Acts, chapter 22, during a situation where he was defending his Judaism and knowledge of it to an angry mob of Jews who had falsely accused him of denying his faith by teaching falsehood and desecrating the Temple. He was charged with being a defector, when what he was risking his life to do was tell them of the true God who had come to His own people.

This is not unlike today where upon your profession of Christ as a Jew you are often labeled a traitor at worst and the very least one who is denying as completely as possible his faith as a Jew. I know. I've heard it and felt it.

The apostle desperately wanted his people to know that he had been wrong all along. To help prove this he presented his credentials as the "Jew of Jews," one who none of them no matter how devout could ever compare to. And then from that point he labored to show them that this was where his devotions should have been, that he knew Judaism better than they, and that what he was telling them was it, it was the fulfillment of all they been taught, grown up with and held so dear. He spent the rest of his life working through the power of the Holy Spirit to have as many people as possible see this truth. He was beaten many times with rods and whips, but his love for his people and his God overcame that. He was willing to die, not for a lie but for what he knew was the truth, for he had witnessed "the Truth" first hand in person. He would travel to a city and go into the synagogue and as the Scriptures tells,

> "And he entered the synagogue and began speaking out boldly for three months, reasoning and persuading them about the kingdom of God" (Acts 19:8).

He was able to do this because the Hebrew Scriptures, the Old Testament, in painstaking detail described and pointed to the Messiah who had come.

I told you of how I can understand the emotions, the pain the apostle Paul felt for his brethren. The passage that strikes me the hardest is found in Romans chapter 9 in the New Testament. Paul writes starting in verse 1:

> "I am telling the truth in Christ, I am not lying, my conscience testifies with me in the Holy Spirit, that I have great sorrow and unceasing grief in my heart. For I could wish that I myself were accursed, separated from Christ for the sake of my brethren, my kinsmen according to the flesh" (Romans 9:1)

His heart is seen in that he was willing to lose the most precious thing he possessed, his very salvation that his people would embrace the truth. His great love for his fellow Jews is shown here, and the great weight on his heart for their salvation that he was willing to be damned himself, to lose his salvation for their sake, so they could be saved. I can tell you there is nothing as difficult as seeing one of your brothers and sisters in the flesh, kinsmen, the Jewish people, members of God's covenant with Israel, part of such a long and great heritage, of a nation God separated out for Himself from all other nations, (Ex. 33:16; Lev. 20:24; 1 Kings 8:53), which was supposed to be His nation to witness to the world reject this reaching out to them by God. There is nothing like seeing one of these reject the very Messiah who they claim is their hope, but has not yet arrived. Through His great love for them He came first to His people. It was told to us by God in the Scriptures, that this rejection would occur, and indeed it did, but it does not stop us from weeping for them.

The Scripture also tells us in many places that this rejection would not be complete, it would not be total. God always preserved a remnant, and told of this in the Hebrew Scriptures, the Old Testament (Gen. 45:7; 2 Kin. 19:4; Ezra 9:8; Is.10:21; Jer. 6:9; Mal. 2:15). What brings great hope is that God promises that as part of His covenant that He made with Israel, He is not done with them. He does generously and mercifully promise a restoration of Israel. Romans 11:2 tells us:

> *God has not rejected His people whom He foreknew. Or do you not know what the Scripture says in the passage about Elijah, how he pleads with God against Israel?*
> LORD, THEY HAVE KILLED YOUR PROPHETS, THEY HAVE TORN DOWN YOUR ALTARS, AND I ALONE AM LEFT, AND THEY ARE SEEKING MY LIFE.

Elijah the prophet thought he was the only faithful Israelite left. But God tells him that this is not so, not all have rejected His ways and gone after "other gods." God had preserved a remnant, those who would still believe. This is quoted by Paul in the New Testament because the situation was similar in his day with his people rejecting his message, which was God's message. But even then God had a remnant. He was proving that He was not done with the Jewish people and that His love and mercy were still upon His beloved chosen people. Chapter 11 of the book of Romans goes on to elaborate about this restoration of the Jewish people and God's completion of His covenant promises to them (Romans 11:1-36).

My daughter had a friend who was Jewish and we quickly became friends with the parents. We would talk with them when we would go to pick up our daughter when they had a play date. Each time we would have a nice visit but the opportunity never arose to share with them about Jesus, and I kept praying God would provide one in the future. Our hearts had always been out for them. As time went by I thought about how we were becoming good friends and how much we enjoyed knowing them but that we had never discussed the Lord. If I truly cared about them I wouldn't allow it to never happen. In this short time here on earth we have to stay focused on the eternity that awaits us. I decided that next time I was there I would just initiate and see what his reaction would be. You never know, you could easily lose a friendship over this, but if you truly love people, you will do it because you care more about their eternal destiny than what they think about you.

We went over one day as he was kind enough to help us with a computer problem we were having. We worked in his office for several hours because as with most computer situations, it took longer than expected. We were developing a good relationship with them and it was always comfortable and easy when we spoke. I wanted to mention that in light of what happened next. When we were done he walked me out to the car and I mentioned to him about a series of letters between a Messianic Jewish man and his Rabbi, and that it was a fascinating exchange. It didn't sound canned or pushy, it just flowed like any normal conversation. When I finished he went completely blank. He said nothing, just stared at me. His countenance completely changed. Then I thought, uh huh, this is awkward. From the look on his face this was going nowhere. I went on as if nothing happened and asked if he might consider listening to it as it was on tape but he shut me down immediately. "No," was all he said. He refused to even talk about it, at all. Since the moment I brought it up his demeanor had completely changed, and it remained that way. He didn't say another word, he had turned to stone. What was odd about it was that during that same day when were in his office, I saw lots of books on the shelves. There were books on Judaism, and some on philosophy, reasoning etc. I thought to myself that this guy will certainly have a lot to say based on what I saw up on his bookshelf. He must have spent some time studying. I figured that he would debate the issue and spiritedly from what I saw on the shelf. I remember thinking to myself, you bring it up and he'll just take it from there. But that was not the case, not at all. Immediately, and unhesitatingly, he ended any chance of conversation. He just said no and goodbye and that was it.

In the car after I left, driving home, I had this profound sense of sadness for him. I just wanted to cry for that family. What good is anything that this world has to offer without being right with God? Anything we gain is lost when we die. That is why Jesus said in Matthew 16:26:

> *"For what will it profit a man if he gains the whole world and forfeits his soul? Or what will a man give in exchange for his soul?"*

When we weigh the importance of anything we ponder in this life our eternal destiny should certainly at the top of any list of priorities.

There was a Jewish man in his seventies whom I became good friends with at the local health club in our small town. It was a close-knit group at that club being in such a small town and we'd all have fun joking with each other and putting off the days troubles. He knew I was a Christian almost right from the start from conversations we had had, but didn't know right away that I was Jewish. When it was the time of year for the Jewish holidays Rosh Hashanah and Yom Kippur, he discovered I was Jewish as well. These holidays naturally came up during conversations because he would not come into the gym at that time and told us why. I told him I was Jewish also, and this inevitably led to a question on his part as to why I was a Christian. I told him because Jesus is the promised Messiah and that this was a fulfillment of my Judaism not an abandonment of it. You know it was funny because as soon as I told him I was Jewish we really hit it off. He was put off by what I told about the Messiah and when I told him that I was writing a book about it he told me he wanted nothing to do with it. But he must have gotten over it because he started telling all kinds of those uniquely Jewish stories like I talked about at the beginning of the book. This man had such an infectious personality and people loved him wherever he went. He was one of those guys who could just look at you and make you laugh. You'd say something he wouldn't agree with and he'd give you one of those looks, looking down over his glasses that he'd drop down as he leaned forward toward you, his eyes locked on you. It was a funny, dubious little look, as I remembered it from living in New York. That made me miss living there and the people I used to know. So we would have a great time and I would love to hear about all of the things that happened in his life over the years; it was great. I would pray for him and again, these prayers for my fellow Jews seemed to surpass any others I would do in intensity.

Although he didn't say much of anything at that point, he did later and even asked questions such as how could I have anything to do with religion because of evil in the world. I told him how the state of our world is the result of our sin (as when we looked at Romans chapter 5:12-21), and that when God made the world He said it was good because it was. There was no problem at first, we caused all the trouble with our sin. God graciously came down here to help a people who made this mess and could not help themselves.

A question such as that would come up and there would usually be a short exchange and then we would go on to something else, he did not want to stay on it for long. But then some time would pass and then we would get back on a religious topic, and remarkably usually at his initiation of it.

One time he said that we should forget about religion and just be nice to each other, that we should disregard all of our differences, meaning religious views, and just get along, and then we'd have peace. He went on to mention the inquisitions and violence in the name of religion. I mentioned how there has been much more violence from nonreligious leaders than religious, that it doesn't even compare. Stalin, Mao, Edie Amine, Poll Pot, Hitler. I said that the people of the Inquisitions were not following Jesus and what He taught, but rather these were people doing their own will, not God's will. I told him briefly that no amount of disregarding anyone's belief is going to solve the problem. If everyone got together and said that they were going to disregard every ideology, even if it was possible it wouldn't solve anything.

Even disregarding all our previous ideologies and starting this new one supposedly with none is an ideology of itself. So it is not even possible. The problem is an individual one, between each man and God. The problem is the very one that Jesus came into the world to solve. The problem is sin. So as I said before we are living in a problem that we created. Our hearts are so far from God that we don't want anything to do with this plan. We follow our own dictates naturally and not His, that's why we invent alternate religions to follow. His way is our only hope. So since the fall of Adam, man is by nature a sinner and will not be able to fix the world situation. He needs God to change his heart before he can do anything good (Romans 3:12). So instead of tossing away the solution, which is Jesus, we need to embrace Him and for all we are worth! He is the only one who can change the hearts of men (Ezekiel 26:36; 2 Corinthians 5:17), and then they will spend eternity with Him.

There were all kinds of memories to share of living "back East," playing stickball against a red brick building, going to local corner shop and having an egg cream soda, ball games at Yankee Stadium, and trips to "the shore." We had so much common and a natural affinity for each other. Our families were often the topic, talking of the holidays and our relatives and all the crazy things they did. We shared a lot about each other's lives, and others in the gym would often be in many conversations but when we talked of things distinctly Jewish, they all seemed to unintentionally meld into the background. We got lost in it. When one of us would share a story it would spark another one in either one of us, each wanting to share as our experiences were so similar.

The large time gap in our ages completely fell away due to our cultural ties. He felt comfortable telling me much about his life, how he missed working and the people he knew, all of the relationships. He said every where he went people knew him. He told stories about them all. He would go on for a time about a man who I felt that at the end of the story I knew personally, and some he would tell had recently died, and I felt the loss.

He seemed no different to me than when he was in his prime that he talked so much about. Our heritage immediately bound us together and as if we had known each other all our lives, but this also made it more painful thinking of the gap that separated us, and my pain for wanting him to enjoy eternal fellowship with his Lord, a Lord that he thought he did know. The worst moment came, and I'll never forget it, the day when we were walking side by side in the gym and He put his arm on my shoulder as went and said to me, "One day we'll get you back." My heart sank. Its one of those things you never get over.

Remember at the beginning of the chapter the apostle Paul spent time proving that he was the quintessential, the model Jew, excelling in all areas beyond his detractors. But he then told of how he was originally on the wrong track and how God graciously showed him the way. We remember before his conversion in the desert how ardently he went after defending the Jewish faith, but he then realized he had all the zeal but without the right knowledge. He wrote about his fellow Jewish brothers who are zealous for their faith. But this zeal is misdirected. Again, his strong heartfelt love for them is seen here. This is in Romans chapter 10 verse 1:

> *Brethren, my hearts desire and my prayer to God for them is for their salvation. For I testify that they have a zeal for God, but not in accordance with knowledge. For not knowing about God's righteousness and seeking to establish their own, they did not subject themselves to the righteousness of God.* (Romans 10:1)

The Jewish people of his time may have been zealous in attempting to keep the Law of God perfectly (which is the requirement to gain entrance into heaven, though no one can do it as Romans 3:23 and other passages tell us), and may have vigorously resisted other religions other than Judaism, but they did this not in accordance with the truth. It was a futile effort. Only the righteousness of Christ appropriated by faith in Him, can give us right standing with God. We cannot seek to establish it ourselves or by our standards as Paul is telling us they tried to.

Paul says, and we have to get a handle on this, he says he knows they are zealous for God, he says my people have a zeal for God, *but* he then talked of the utmost necessity of this zeal being connected with the truth. Many people are sincerely devoted to certain beliefs, but they can, as the Bible shows here, be sincerely mistaken. This caused great pain for the apostle then, as it does for me now, and I am sure for my fellow Jewish believers in Jesus the Messiah for their brethren who do not.

My people and I grew up loving the same heritage, praying the same prayers, reciting the Shema, hearing the Torah. They feel that they truly love and know the great and holy God of Israel, the God who came down to speak with Moses on Mt. Sinai and I feel the most profound sadness, the deepest sadness because it is not possible. I wish so badly for them to be saved. They think I have strayed, they want me to come back to them as my friend told me. It is so tough, because they are the ones who need to come back. They see me as away from the dear God that we grew up revering, who took us out of the world and made His people, who rescued us from the bondage in Egypt, after hearing our cry. We celebrated this every year at the Passover. Every young Jew experienced sitting at the Seder table, while the father proudly looks on, as part of the great tradition of the youngest son carrying it on, asking the four questions, reading Hebrew, during the Seder service, starting with asking why is this night different from all other nights? We would practice all day long for this event memorizing the portion we were to read that night. We celebrated our freedom and God's mercy.

This is not necessary anymore as Jesus is our great Passover. Just as in Egypt the blood of the lamb saved us from death. We were "passed over" by the angel of death, passed over only the homes of the Jews who put the blood of the lamb over their doorposts. This was the only way to escape the angel of death who was coming to smite the Egyptians. Jesus is the Lamb of God and through His blood alone we escape death. The old Passover is gone, the new has come. Jesus said to His disciples as they celebrated the Passover the night before He was to go to the cross, He changed the service, one that had stood for centuries upon centuries. He said, "This cup which is poured out for you is the new covenant in My blood." As God had promised, the Messiah had come and now as God had said in Jeremiah 31:31 God was making a new covenant with His people, not like the old. God promised to forgive their sins, to remember them no more. This was fulfilled in Jesus, the Messiah. As the Jews in the old Passover put the blood across their doorposts and believed it would save them, so we trust in the blood of Christ, the spotless Lamb of God, shed for us. God will certainly "passover" and preserve all who put their trust in this.

Oh that I could impart that knowledge of the truth to them but that is all under the province of the Holy Spirit, who is all wise. I must trust in the wisdom and sovereignty of God to handle all of the affairs of the universe and just concentrate on being obedient to Him and doing what He has called me to do. I must trust in God to do everything else.

Any view that I take departing from that takes glory from the One who deserves all glory, our Lord God omnipotent.

They want me to come back to God, they say. But they can't love God, without loving Jesus, or have the Father and reject the Son. The passages are numerous (John 5:23; 37-38; 8:19; 8:42; 12:48-50; 14:7; 15:20-21,23; 16:2-3). He said if you indeed loved the Father you would love Me, for He sent Me. When I pray for my Jewish brothers and sisters I can't help but be struck with the thought, "Why me? How am I one of the remnant that He spoke of that would believe while so many rejected the Messiah when He came? (Romans 11:5). There was nothing I could do, for we are all saved by God's grace, an unmerited gift, as it says in Ephesians 2:8-9:

> *For by grace you have been saved through faith; and that not of yourselves, it is the gift of God; not as a result of works, so that no one may boast.*

We are told that our salvation is an undeserved gift, given to us by God through faith or trust in Him. We are further told that this is not because of any good things we have done, but it is solely a work of God and therefore there is nothing that a person can boast about in regards to their salvation. Jesus came to this earth to do for us what we cannot do, be good enough to enter into heaven and repair the relationship with God that our sin destroyed. Only His goodness is good enough. We put our trust in that and it is applied to us, we have this righteousness accounted to us and the problem is solved. We are made right with God and are then able to spend an eternity with Him as a free gift of His mercy not according to anything we could have done. Once someone tries to makes entrance to heaven a man-made thing they will not measure up (Romans 3:23 says that all have sinned and fall short of the glory of God). For if we try that we are also not talking about grace anymore, we're talking about earning it. Grace, the unmerited gift, and earning or working toward something, are antithetical. You either have one or the other. Romans 11:6 makes this clear to us when it says:

> *But if it is by grace, it is no longer on the basis of works, otherwise grace is no longer grace.*

We have to realize most importantly that our salvation is of God, there is nothing we can do in and of ourselves. 1 Corinthians 1:30-31 says:

> *But by His doing you are in Christ Jesus, who became to us wisdom from God, and righteousness and sanctification, and redemption, so that, just as it is written,* "LET HIM WHO BOASTS, BOAST IN THE LORD."

Romans 4:1-3 tell us:

> *What then shall we say that Abraham, our forefather according to the flesh, has found? For if Abraham was justified by works, he has something to boast about, but not before God. For what does the Scripture say?* ABRAHAM BELIEVED GOD, AND IT WAS CREDITED TO HIM AS RIGHTEOUSNESS.

Abraham is talked about here. If we think the apostle Paul was the Jew of Jews, how about Abraham? He is called the father of the Jewish nation. Abraham was saved because he believed in God's plan in sending His Messiah, and believing in that alone, in the righteousness of the Righteous One, was the only reason, not anything he alone did is the crucial point. Virtually every religion tries to reach up to God in some way. God's way was to reach down to a helpless people and offer them a righteousness they did not have.

I am Jewish and although we're called God's chosen people, we're chosen for His own possession. He said he choose us not because we were the most in number than any other people, but rather for we were as He says, "the least of all peoples" (Deuteronomy 7:6-8). It was purely out of His mercy. It had nothing to do with us, our goodness, or what we did. God did this out of His great love and faithfulness to the promises He made to our fathers, the patriarchs, as He did with Abraham first. In Romans chapter three we are told that all are under sin, all have fallen short of God's glory, Jew and Greek, or Jew or non-Jew. But Romans three also tells us that was an advantage to being a Jew, and said very much so indeed. But you ask, "Why, if we are all under sin and all just as much need a Savior." What's the advantage? This is because we had the oracles of God. We were privileged to be given the Word of God, His very thoughts to know, to hold, and to study. We had in our hands, in our care, the message of salvation itself. We were privileged to know the King of Kings, the Lord of Lords. The One who created the and sustains all of the universe dwelled with us, literally, "tabernacled" with us. He "pitched His tent" with us, which is the literal meaning of His dwelling with His people.

We are all saved the same way, the Old Testament Jew who was saved, looked toward the Messiah to come, and the New Testament Christian looks back to what He has done. But the ancient Jew knew this before Christ came, before breakthrough of the kingdom of God upon this world. The Jew never had the fellowship with God that you do on this side of the cross. Coming from the OT side of the cross as a Jew helped make me really feel the weight of what we have in Christ.

8

Our Witness to the Jewish People

A discussion was once brought up in a group that I was leading about how once we are saved by God and are believers in Christ, He doesn't just immediately transport us to heaven to dwell with Him. We talked about how we stay here for a time, and that we are here for a purpose. (This is covered more extensively in my book, Calling All Christians in the first chapter entitled, Our Best Day).We are created first and foremost to glorify God (Isaiah 43:7; Matthew 5:16; 1 Corinthians 10:31, and others), and one of the ways we will accomplish this is in evangelism. His great mercy and love is shown in the redemption of His people, and we have the privilege of being used as instruments in His hand for His work. We are here to be used by Him to complete the great commission as given by Jesus in Matthew 28:19-20. Jesus said:

> *"Go therefore and make disciples of all the nations, baptizing them in the name of the Father, and the Son, and the Holy Spirit, teaching them to observe all that I commanded you; and lo, I am with you always, even to the end of the age."*

After God does the work of salvation for us we are sent out to tell of the good news of the salvation found in Jesus Christ. We are so grateful to have received this greatest of gifts by the mercy of God, and now, we are commissioned to be used by God to tell others. When we have a situation where we can discuss this with someone who is not in a saving relationship with God we are anxious to tell them, we want them to be saved as well. We will not always get a positive response, in fact, most of the time you probably won't. This is expected as 1 Corinthians 1:18; 2:14 tell us. We know as believers that unless the Holy Spirit works supernaturally to open the eyes of someone, they will not see, and not be saved (see John chapter three as an example). But we witness to people, we tell them, anyway, because though the providence of God is not our purview, only God can save someone, we have the privilege of being used by God to deliver His message of salvation (Romans 10:14). When someone doesn't respond we are sad for them. There are times when I share the gospel with someone and they don't respond, and at least as far as I can see, because you don't know what will happen after you leave. When they don't respond I want to weep for them right there.

What then do we do with what we know? What is our response once we know and embrace through God's grace this message of salvation wrought by the coming of the Messiah? God has ordained that we be used as tools in His hand to tell people about it, to share the gospel, or good news. The word gospel literally means "good news." We are to be the "light of the world." We are to reflect the love of God to others, and spread the message of salvation, and fulfill our goal in life of glorifying God. We are not to huddle amongst ourselves, rather through our shining example lead people to the Lord.

> *"You are the light of the world. A city on a hill cannot be hidden; nor does anyone light a lamp and put it under a basket, but on the lampstand, and it gives light to all who are in the house. Let your light shine before men in such a way that they may see your good works, and glorify your Father who is in heaven."* (Matthew 5:14-16)

Why is this message so important? Why is the act of our telling people this so integrally tied to our love for them? Why did I say that I weep for my people when they wouldn't hear it and did not acknowledge the Messiah who came and along with Him salvation?

It is because anyone without it is without hope. The apostle Paul wrote in Ephesians 2:12 that those without Christ are without hope. He goes on to say that He is our peace. Romans 5:1 says,

Therefore, having been justified by faith, we now have peace with God through our Lord Jesus Christ.

The chapter goes on to describe how all of this happened that we would need a Savior in the first place. In verse 12 of chapter 5 it says,

Therefore, just as through one man sin entered into the world, and death through sin, and so death spread to all men, because all sinned. (Romans 5:12)

So here we have our problem, sin. Our sin separated us from God. We are then left estranged from him and cannot have fellowship with Him in heaven. God is perfectly holy and cannot even look upon sin (Habakkuk 1:13), and no unclean thing, compared to God, such as all of us, can enter into the kingdom of heaven (Revelation 21:27).

We have to remember that when God made us He said it was good, (Genesis 1:31)

We had right fellowship with Him. Our choice to sin is what has caused the whole problem to begin with just as we saw in Romans 5:12. The penalty of sin is death (Romans 6:23), and eternal separation from God (2 Thessalonians 1:7-9; Matthew 25:41). We needed a Savior who would live the perfect life, obeying God's Laws perfectly, as we were supposed to, and be our place.

Not only that, but God is perfectly righteous, and consequently He is perfect in His judgments (Job 34:10-12). Therefore, He is a perfect judge. No crimes that were committed could be let go. We may be able to compromise righteousness and just let it go, but God cannot. He is altogether righteous and uncontaminated by sin, and as the book of Habakkuk told us God is too pure to look upon evil or let it go when an offense has been made (Habakkuk 1:13). A perfect judge demands perfect justice. In God's eyes our sin is evil, it is a moral crime to break anyone of God's Laws. So we also need someone who could also take all of the punishment on himself that we have incurred, from breaking

God's Law (which is the standard, and perfect keeping of it, Galatians 3:10; Deuteronomy 27:26, which Jesus did for us Romans 5:13-21). So we need a Savior to satisfy divine justice, and make us right with God to give us peace with God.

Now we are back to Romans chapter five verse one.

Who else could have done this? God provided a way back to Him. If people don't accept that, they will not accept anything in its place (Luke 16: 27-31), even a person coming back from the dead to tell them as the verse explains. So creating many ways would not solve the problem. What should be most amazing is that God provided "a" way at all back to Him. This way was given purely out of His mercy toward us as we are totally incapable of saving ourselves. Jesus is the only one because He is the only One who could have done it. He was without sin (2 Corinthians 5:21), had broken no laws of God. He came to be sin for us, to act in our behalf, to be treated as if He Himself, although perfect and holy, committed these crimes against God and then He took all of the punishments deserved on Himself. He is the Lamb of God who takes away the sins of the world. (John 1:29).

I know I have been talking over and over again in this book about my concern for my fellow Jewish people. And I have said how one of the things that adds to my feelings of lament for them is that the Messiah came here first for them. Jesus is for them as an answer to the promises made to the Jewish people by God. When Jesus sent out His apostles on an evangelistic mission He gave them the following instructions.

In verse 5-7 of chapter 10 of Matthew's gospel:

> *These twelve Jesus sent out after instructing them: "Do not go in the way of the Gentiles, and do not enter any city of the Samaritans; but rather go to the lost sheep of the house of Israel. And as you go, preach, saying, 'The kingdom of heaven is at hand.'" (Matthew 10:5-7)*

And in chapter 15 of Matthew, starting at verse 21:

> *Jesus went away from there, and withdrew into the district of Tyre of Sidon. And a Canaanite woman from that*

> region came out and began to cry out, saying, "Have mercy on me, Lord, Son of David; my daughter is cruelly demon-possessed."
>
> But He did not answer her a word. And His disciples came and implored Him, saying, "Send her away, because she keeps shouting at us."
>
> But He answered and said, "I was sent only to the lost sheep of the house of Israel."
>
> But she came and began to bow down before Him, saying, "Lord, help me!" (Matthew 15:21-25)

Jesus did indeed help her, answering her request and healing her daughter, but it is important to see why He initially sent her away. He said that He was here for the lost sheep of Israel. He came for the Jews. The Mission of the Messiah was to first come for the Jewish people in fulfillment of the promises, the prophecies in the Old Testament. When Jesus was about to ascend back to heaven He commissioned the apostles to go to the rest of the world and spread the message of salvation through Christ, but first the Messiah was here for His people, the Jews.

Jesus instructed His disciples to go back to Jerusalem and wait for the power of the Holy Spirit to come upon them to equip them for the special service they were about to do

(We are all equipped by the Holy Spirit for acts of service. This is not the same as the regenerating gift of the Spirit that Jesus talked of in John chapter three, this is the baptism of the Spirit that every believer receives to equip him to serve God upon their salvation). Once they received this gift they were to go out from Jerusalem and tell the world of the gift of salvation from God. So Jesus came for His people, the Jewish people, then He commissioned the apostles to spread the message out from there radiating outward until, with all believers fulfilling their commission, spreading out across the entire world.

> So when they had come together, they were asking Him, saying, "Lord is it at this time that You are restoring the kingdom to Israel?" He said to them, "It is not for you to know times or epochs which the Father has fixed by His

own authority; but you will receive power when the Holy Spirit has come upon you; and you shall be My witnesses both in Jerusalem, and in all Judea and Samaria, and even to the remotest parts of the earth. (Acts 1:6:8)

This job is still going on today and will continue until the return of the Lord, and is the obligation of every believer. Jesus gave all of His believers what is called the great commission.

"Go therefore and make disciples of all of the nations, baptizing them in the name of the Father and the Son and the Holy Spirit, teaching them to observe all that I commanded you; and lo, I am with you always, even to the end of the age." (Matthew 28:19-20)

When sharing this with Jewish people they may say that this whole business of this message to the Jews being for everyone is not in the Old Testament. This is a common assertion, people thinking we are presenting some new teaching, but this is anything but new. This was the same situation the apostle Paul encountered in his day, writing in the first century. In verse 1 of Romans chapter 1:

Paul, a bond-servant of Christ Jesus, called as an apostle, set apart for the gospel of God. (Romans 1:1)

The apostle is talking of the gospel of God, that he was appointed directly by Christ for this task of spreading the message of salvation. He then goes on to tell how this was first presented by the prophets of the Old Testament, that this is nothing new. Many Jewish people of the apostles' day saw his preaching as antagonistic to the Jewish religion, but he presents here that it is anything but that. They saw it as some new teaching antithetical to their beliefs. But as we have seen it is a fulfillment of the promises of God.

1:2 *which He promised beforehand through the prophets in the Holy Scriptures* (Romans 1:2)

This presents the great truth that this presentation of the gospel is not something new but is a fulfillment, a completion of promises made in OT, mysterious and hidden, now revealed. This is a crucial point that needed to be made to Jews that this was from God and subsequently from the Old Testament, not from men but from God, not new, but old.

God's plan was not something new, or that He changed course, it was planned before the foundation of the world. The Jews saw this teaching of the apostle Paul as something new and a violation of the law of Moses. They didn't see it for what it is, the completion of their own cherished beliefs. Ephesians 1:9 points to this mystery which was hidden and is now revealed:

> *He has made known to us the mystery of His will, according to His kind intention which He purposed in Him. (Ephesians 1:9)*

We now know that we can be reconciled to God through the work of Jesus Christ in our behalf. We see in the unveiling of this mystery what it means to us, and for our future with God in verses 3-5 of Ephesians chapter 1: (we are truly blessed!)

> *Blessed be the God and Father of our Lord Jesus Christ, who has blessed us with every spiritual blessing in the heavenly places in Christ, just as He chose us in Him before the foundation of the world, that we would holy and blameless before Him. In love He predestined us to adoption as sons through Jesus Christ to Himself, according to the kind intention of His will. (Ephesians 1:3-5)*

The very prophets who delivered their message to the ancestors of the Jews of Paul's day were rejected by the people. They were delivering a message that began with a promise, a promise of the incredible redemption that God would provide according to the kind intention of His will. The Jews certainly saw Moses as a great prophet. As Jesus said in John 5:46-47:

For if you believed Moses, you would believe Me, for he wrote of Me. But if you do not believe his writings, how will you believe My words?

So the things that are recorded in the New Testament are all foreshadowed and predicted to come true in the Old Testament. So all of the predictions of who the Messiah would be and what He would do, as we saw in the chapter on the Messiah-ship of Jesus, hold up, but there is more. The whole plan of redemption that God had ordained before the foundation of the world did also see their realization in the New Testament. God did make these promises in the past in the Old Testament. This whole plan of salvation that we see in the New Testament was indeed what Romans 1:2 says, was **"promised beforehand through the prophets in the Holy Scriptures."** Just as the apostle Paul had to explain to the Jewish people of his day we have to explain now, this teaching of Christianity is nothing new or different, it is the fulfillment of Judaism. God promises to the Jews of the coming Messiah have occurred, as well as His inclusion of the Gentiles, or non-Jews, in His plan of salvation.

We see this prophecy of the inclusion of the Gentiles in the plan of salvation in the book of Hosea.

This is so critical for Jewish people to see this. A major objection to Christianity, to the acceptance of Jesus as Messiah and Lord is that this is all something new and a perversion of the old. Having people see the "Jewish-ness" of the Christian message is essential. And essential is a good term to describe it because Christianity would have no basis without it, or to put it another way, no foundation at all without the Jewish Scriptures. The predictions of the Messiah are, as we have seen, perfectly fulfilled in Jesus, and it is not possible for anyone else to have done it. We have seen how modern rabbinical thought in an attempt to distance Judaism from Christianity has gone against the body of historical rabbinical thought and interpretation. Christian interpretation of Messianic passages in the Scriptures agree with the tradition of rabbinical knowledge. It also agrees with rabbinical interpretations and modern Jews need to see this so they are not kept from the truth. This can't be stressed enough in terms of witnessing to them, for you will be seen as someone trying to pull them away from all they have been thought and they have loved.

It is a very common to hear a Jewish person say, "Well then why do so many reject Jesus as Messiah?" As we have seen this is in agreement with the prophecies of the Messiah some of which we looked at previously such as Isaiah fifty three. God talks to us in His Word about this rejection, so this just strengthens the testimony of the Scriptures in the New Testament. Also we have to keep this in mind when witnessing because rejection will be much more the norm than acceptance and openness to the message. So don't lose heart, we are here to give the message, changing the heart is the business of God. The outcome of our witnessing is of the Lord. But through His sovereign decree He chooses to use us as the means, a tool in His hands. No matter what the reaction is we should eagerly look for opportunities to do this out of our love for people and our wish to see them saved.

But in doing this we need to be all things to all people. This means that we witness according to the situation and the direction of the discussion. We respond to opportunities and create opportunities when appropriate. If someone is a practicing Jew with training in the Talmud for example, the approach and conversation will be completely different than someone who is also Jewish but does not go to temple and is not familiar with the Old Testament. There is also the person who not only does not go worship in a temple but is Jewish by ethnicity and is does not hold to the truth of the Old Testament and considers it little more binding than any other "mythological story."

For the person who does hold to the teachings of the Old Testament and is perhaps learned in the Scriptures, your answer would be akin to much of the information presented in previous chapters of this book and similar works. This response would be much more heavily based on more technical information, dealing with issues such as the quotes of the early rabbis in relation to Christian teaching for example. Much more likely though is the Jewish person who does not know very much of the Old Testament and then it will be up to you to present the point of views of the Old and New Testament and show that they are not in conflict. But again, the response you present has to fit the situation and the knowledge level of the person you are talking to. If you come out with too much information or talk at a level that is far above the knowledge of the person they will absorb little or nothing of what you are trying to convey, and will probably not seek you out again for information. Remember the goal. It is not to show what you know or win an argument, it is to be faithful to the great commission that Jesus gave us in Matthew twenty eight.

Movies and popular literature frequently paint Christian missionaries as cold, calculating, wicked people, who work to convert people by any means possible. You see them cruelly forcing people into their ways, seemingly destroying these people innate views, beliefs that seem suited for them, "because it doesn't matter what they believe anyway." The entire process is seen as coercive, and heartless. I have heard people say "How could they take them from what they have learned all their lives, how bigoted and inconsiderate."

If Jesus is indeed correct which He is shown to be, the worst thing a person could do is not tell someone of the truth for their salvation. And if someone did act like the Hollywood characterizations, and I am not doubting that there are some people who do just that, they are not following the mandates of Jesus, but have gone off on their own and will be culpable for their actions. People are supposed to see the "light" of Christ in our lives (Matthew 5:14-16), a love that is so completely different from the rest of the world, and be attracted to it, never forceful, never coercive. The force is in the message itself, and a life that is lived the way Jesus intended us to. This type of life blows people away and shows how we love them.

You may have to work on dispelling such myths first and not going into all kinds of proofs for the truth. It may be by demonstrating your excellent behavior and unusual interest for them that most good will be seen. Certainly, if our behavior is not as exemplary as it should be people will be quick to bring this out and will not give much credence to your presentation of the gospel. The apostle Peter wrote of how exceptional our lives as Christians should be, and how the result will be the glory of God.

> *Keep your behavior excellent among the Gentiles, so that in the thing in which they slander you as evildoers, they*

> *may because of your good deeds, as they observe them, glorify God in the day of visitation* (1 Peter 2:12).

A good example or rule of thumb to follow is if something theological is brought up and you are asked to respond to a question, do that and then say no more. If there is an objection to what you just said keep going giving a further response. Try to keep your responses as concise as possible. Work on being clear and not overbearing. Be zealous in your desire for evangelism but not overzealous in your presentation. We should display our great joy in Christ but not scare people away. You also have to be acutely aware of the interest level of the person. Don't ignore this or you will run off on your own and not be catering to the needs of the situation. You are there to do the job God has called you to do and care to the needs of that person. Don't withhold information they need to hear but just do it in a way that is sensitive to them and the situation.

So stay within the bound of the circumstance, and I will give examples to follow, and stay within the interest level or active attention they will devote to you. The goal is to be a winsome ambassador for Christ and being there to fulfill the mandate God has provided or else you can easily overwhelm people and end any contact with them in the future. This also illustrates the need for Christians to be learned in all areas pertaining to the faith, so we can answer questions in a wide variety of situations, and be used more by the Lord for His purposes. They we can carry out the mandate of 1 Peter 3:15:

> *But sanctify Christ as Lord in your hearts, always being ready to make a defense to everyone who asks you to give an account for the hope that is in you, yet with gentleness and reverence.* (1 Peter 3:15)

Being ready is paramount here. Many people don't see the necessity of diligent study of the things of our faith, especially knowing the Word of God well, this is one of them. How can we witness about things of God without having a solid grasp of His word. If we don't, we won't know who our God is, and what He expects of us either. We are to give a defense, we are to stand for the truth (Jude 1:3), but how we do it is everything. What is in our hearts is reflected by how we speak and act. Think of what it says about us and what is going on in our hearts when the reason we are so desirous to answer someone is because of our pride, perhaps to win the argument instead of winning someone to Christ for an eternity. Or what does it say of us if we detest a person because they disagree with us instead of feeling sorrowful because they don't have the truth, and without God they are lost. So if we are not following the guidelines of the Holy Spirit and speaking to people about Christ with gentleness and reverence we are not being obedient to Christ and following His teachings, and we are displaying the callousness of our own hearts.

And as we are told any knowledge we have without love is useless (1 Corinthians 13:1-2). We need to look inward and see a love or burden for lost people is there, if not why?

The whole enterprise of witnessing is off course if you are trying to win an argument or feed or maintain your pride. Then you need to take serious stock of your spiritual condition. When witnessing with a proper heart your care, your concern, your love will come through. This must be hand-in-hand with the message we give.

While working at a physical therapy clinic there was a patient who came in, an older Jewish woman, who we will call Gloria. Her treatment course was long and this afforded a lot of time for a relationship to form between us. It was so nice because we had developed a genuine friendship and she knew that I had her best interest at heart.

The irony of the situation was that when the opportunity actual came to witness to her the time I actually had to speak to her was exceedingly short. I had been praying for quite some time for an opportunity to share with her, but one had not come up. This clinic was very serious about infringing upon someone with sharing of beliefs and made that very clear. They knew however that I was a Christian and took my faith seriously, but it didn't present a problem by respecting their wishes while still remaining faithful to the calling of Matthew 28:19-20 and Acts 1:8 about being God's witnesses to the remotest parts of the earth.

This situation with the guidelines of the clinic toward this type of discussion about religion wound up being the most powerful witness

THE MOST JEWISH THING I COULD DO

that presented itself. They told me that they were originally nervous about my being a Christian and my commitment to it when they hired me. They said that they had experienced problems in the past with a Christian employee and their inappropriate and overzealous proselytizing. At the time they thought all Christians were a bit wacko. But this gave me the chance to explain to them about how we are to be in subjection to the authority we are under as long as they are not asking us to disobey God. I got to talk about proper witnessing and how Christ wanted us to act. This owner who had been so strongly negative in regards to Christians began to change his viewpoint and the stereotype was disappearing.

The most important element of this is that it will change his viewpoint of the One we represent. We either will honor Him or drag His perfect name in the mud. The owner then began to ask me all sorts of questions about the faith as a result.

Through all of this I never had the opportunity to talk with Gloria. I continued to pray about it, and one day, when we were extremely busy, and were running, I had put her in a treatment room to put heat on her injury which was the start of her treatment there. We only have about two minutes to do this as when we are that busy, because you have to move fast and keep moving to not disturb the flow, as patients are constantly coming in and moving from area to area.

When I was putting on her hot-packs she asked me a question. She said, "How do you and your wife handle the fact that you are Jewish and she is a Christian?" There it was, my opportunity. The thing was I knew I only had about a minute and a half to do it, anything longer would disturb the flow and affect everyone at work, and we'd get behind. If I just stayed in there I'm sure the boss would certainly be upset at me for just sitting in there and talking to her. So I prayed quickly for the Holy Spirit to please help me with a brief "schpeel," as we so often say in Jewish circles. And if need be, the Lord would provide another opportunity and maybe with someone else.

So in a about minute or so I told her of how it was the most natural thing for us because the Jewish religion is very much focused on the promised Messiah, and my wife is as well. Jesus fulfilled all of the hundreds of prophecies concerning the coming of the Messiah, all of which could never be fabricated, you couldn't fake where you would be born and the miraculous element of it, virgin born, what you would do, how you would die, and by a method not even invented yet but predicted by God in the Old Testament book of Isaiah. I added that ancient rabbis agree with modern Christian interpretation of Messianic prophecy. The New Testament displays the same supernatural qualities of the Old, and flows perfectly with it. I told her I would love to talk with her more about this some time if she wanted to and had some good books on this as well that I think she would like if she wanted to read them, smiled, said that I will see her in a little while and left.

In contrast, there was a woman that I had been talking to on and off at my work for many months. And one particular day she was acting very inquisitive and was pressing with questions that showed she was really desiring to get answers. It was all in the context of a relative who had recently died in her family, and as our discussion progressed it moved to one of a more serious nature. She had for the first time begun to ask very probing theological questions.

This time I was self-employed and working one-on-one with my clients. I still had to be sensitive to the other people who were sharing the workspace and to the owner who we all leased the space from, who in turn had his clients there as well. But I saw where this conversation was going and didn't want to inhibit the need that was there, so decided to let the conversation go on. This conversation used up the last five minutes of her session and fifteen of my next client's session. This provides an example of the importance of discernment and how this situation differs from the last. This time I was in charge primarily, even though I still had to use discretion with the owner of the facility and others who used it. Also, I knew the next client that was waiting was a very easy-going fellow who I didn't think would be too upset about my being late for him. I had never been late for him before (an example of how we are to always do our best in whatever we do and the potential ramifications of that) and was willing to risk his being offended by what I was doing because of the manner of her questions.

If he could stomp out or drop me as a client, which I knew was possible, especially since we were sitting right there talking in plain sight of him, thinking I didn't care about him watching and waiting. I thought risking that in this instance was the thing to do, and I knew if I was doing that with the right intentions and followed what was the biblical mandate applied here, God would honor it and I would leave it to Him and not worry about the outcome. If I did that however inappropriately I shouldn't expect God to bless that however. This again is another reason why we have to be so familiar with the Word of God that we can be discerning and make right decisions. This coupled with our constant prayers, also always in line with His Word and not going off on some bizarre tangent, will lead in the right direction. It did turn out alright, as he was not upset and did continue to work with me. This woman and her husband came to church with me after a year and half of invitation, and both gave their lives to Christ.

So you do have to take care of how much you say and when, dependant on the place you work. Some workplace environments are extremely sensitive to discussions of this nature so you have act appropriately. I once received some great advice from an endearing veteran saint when we were talking about witnessing in the workplace. She told us of a man who had been fired from four different jobs because of his witnessing on the job. From what she had told us he apparently was not doing this appropriately, because although we are to be bold in our witness we are not to defy the authority structure. We are called to be witnesses, but not in an inappropriate manner. It takes discernment to know the difference. You have to be aware of the sensitivity of the environment you work in. God will provide opportunities to speak, so don't worry about that. The message of the gospel is offensive to those who are not being saved (1 Peter 2:7-8; 1 Corinthians 1:18, 23; 2:14), and that is unavoidable for us, it is called a stumbling block, a rock of offense, but there is a world of difference between the message of God being offensive to people and giving offense by our behavior. Some people act in an obnoxious or inappropriate manner and then when people act offended they claim they are suffering for Christ. When we do that we are dishonoring God by not being a reflection of His character.

> *Submit yourselves for the Lord's sake to every human institution, whether to a king as the one in authority.* (1 Peter 2:13)

> *Every person is to be in subjection to the governing authorities. For there is no authority except form God, and those which exist are established by God.* (Romans 13:1)

We are under these authorities, which could never exist if God hadn't allowed them to, unless they are telling you to do something contrary to God's will. We also have to remember that the authority at the time of these writings were Roman and perhaps the most harsh in all history, so our job today is nothing like the one they had then. Governments will have to answer to God to how they use the power given to them, but some form of government is still better than none at all, which would lead to anarchy.

So in Gloria's case there was little time, so deep explanation wasn't possible; if there was more time further details can be presented. If the situation doesn't present that time don't force it. Some people don't want a lot of information, some do. Sometimes you may be planting a seed, and you may meet again, if you don't have time then present what you can. Patience is important. This goes right along with truly caring for people, because then you will be patient, you will not give up on them, and over the long haul you'll be there for them and not just want to give them the message once and run. Relationship and trust built and grown over a long period of time provides the best atmosphere for witnessing to someone of the truth. But we can't forget that we are here to care for them also and not witness alone. This again should be natural, further evidence of a changed heart.

But remember that God can and will use any situation He deems right to bring a person to Himself, but we should react appropriately to each one as His instruments, His hands and feet. I was talking to a woman at the front desk who was leaving after her therapy appointment and we got into a conversation about religion, Christianity specifically. She objected to it but the first thing that came out of her mouth was the story of a Christian man that she had met at her office where she worked. She said how rude he was and when they would ask him questions he'd get angry at them. All the while he had his Christian radio station on while he worked. This had a big impact on her. She thought the whole thing was untrue and the thing that stuck out the most was this man's behavior. When a Christian does this he gives offence to people in the name of One who is altogether holy and righteous. When we do that we dishonor God instead of glorifying Him, which is our main purpose for being here (Isaiah 43:7; Matthew 5:16; 1 Corinthians 10:31).

So we want to answer people based on, as the expression goes, "where they are coming from," or how it comes up, and think about meeting their needs and not following an agenda. Jewish people need to see that we care about them, and how what we are presenting is not some new and divergent teaching but a wonderful fulfillment of what they have longed for, the coming of the Messiah. They so desperately need to know how the Messiah came for them and wept over their rejection of Him, although this was predicted in the Word of God, both in the Old and New Testaments, lamented over His people who He came to save but would not hear Him. We are to feel this same way when the message we present falls on deaf ears.

What is most important is that we convey the truth that the God of Judaism is the God who came for them and died on Calvary, on the cross. He is the God who lovingly came down to this world and divested Himself of the glory He deserves as God and suffered in their place (Philippians 2:5-8) as Messiah Ben Joseph was promised to us in Isaiah fifty three of the righteous One who will justify the many as He will bear their iniquities (Isaiah 53:11). He is the God who fought for them and made them victorious in their journey to the land of milk and honey, the Promise Land. He is the same God who brought them out of Egypt. This is the same God we mentioned above that wept over them when approaching Jerusalem over their disobedience. When the Holy Spirit opens people's eyes to this truth it is amazing. This was my experience and I remember feeling the weight of this connection and the gratitude that washed over me.

We need to present the love that our God has for us, and how He has come as promised and could never fail us. We need to present this to our Jewish brothers and sisters. His remnant (those who are Jewish but will believe) will hear His voice and see the depth of God's mercy in not giving up on His people although they have strayed from Him so many times, and although they have disobeyed Him so many times. This is the thing that gets me more than anything else in my own life, is how God stuck with me. I can't believe He hadn't disregarded me although I am certainly unworthy of Him. But in His great mercy, He does regard me. Psalm 8:1, 3-4 says:

> *O Lord, our Lord, how majestic is Your name in all the earth, who have displayed Your splendor above the heavens!*
> *When I consider Your heavens, the work of Your fingers, the moon and the stars, which You have ordained ;*
> <u>*What is man that You take thought of Him, and the son of man that you care for him?*</u> (Psalm 8:1, 3-4)

This is the thing that has evoked so much wonder in me. And when God allowed me to be able to make the connection between all that I had grown up hearing about, all of the stories that stirred awe in me, and how they all pointed to the exalted Messiah who I now knew and loved, I knew I was right with God. I knew who He was and what He had done for me. In Him I could never be lost with no hope of salvation. I knew I would spend eternity in heaven with Him.

My fellow Jewish people need to see that there is no threat from what we are saying.

Rather, they need to know the beauty and completeness upon seeing the promise God made to Abraham being fulfilled and contained in Christ. This is the most wondrous experience for a person imaginable. This is not some new or radical teaching, it is not a departure, but a fulfillment. Jesus said, "Your father Abraham rejoiced to see My day" in John 8:56. Way back in Genesis 15 Abraham was told by God toward the heavens, and to count the stars, as many stars as there were so would his descendants be (Genesis 15:5). The Scripture further tells us that Abraham believed God, He trusted in this promise (Genesis 15:6). God later told him that through his seed the whole world would be blessed (Genesis 22:18). Abraham put his trust in this, and at that moment in Genesis 15:6, he was justified before God. At that moment Abraham was made right before God. His sin he had at the moment no longer separated him from fellowship with God. From the faith that God gave Abraham he was able to trust in the promises of God and then as the Bible says, it was credited him as righteousness. Abraham from that moment on was saved and was going to spend eternity in heaven with God.

What Abraham believed in was the coming of the future redeemer, the Messiah. Jesus said that Abraham rejoiced at seeing Him (John 8:56). Abraham saw the fulfillment of all that God had promised him.

This connection is strong, intertwined throughout the Old Testament, but we need to present this to the Jewish people and pray for God to open their eyes to see it. With love we need to show how the promises that were given to Abraham are given to all of Christ's sheep wherever they are. The same God who thundered on Sinai, and parted the seas for His people to escape from the Pharaoh's army, calmed the storm on the Sea of Galilee as the disciples all sat in the boat frightened out of their minds. He is the same God who raised Lazarus from the dead and can awaken us to spiritual life through faith in His Messiah, the Lord and Savior Jesus Christ.

This ties with and adds weight to the fear that Jewish people think by following Jesus they won't be Jewish anymore. And I had heard and read about many Rabbis and others Jewish people telling their people this very thing. They think they won't be Jews anymore, but this goes back to the title of the book. This is the reason I called this book what I did. I did that because it is truly the most Jewish thing I could do. And that is what our main task is to bring to the Jewish people.

As the apostle Paul went out full of love for his people and so grateful to know the truth and serve the Master, so should we, wherever we are, whether at the workplace or marketplace, home or abroad. This should be our meat and drink if we indeed are grateful for the salvation we now have in Christ and care for others who don't.

And thinking again back to the Tabernacle and all of the doors that prohibited entrance to each stage of access toward God that no man could cross and live, Jesus said in John 10;

> *"I am the door; if anyone enters through Me, he will be saved."* (John 10:7)

Jesus also said, I am the Way, the Truth, and the Life, and no one gets to the Father but through Him. Here is the way, there can be no other. No one could do what He has done. Enter through the door.

There is no other way in. Jesus also said in Matthew chapter 7

> "Enter through the narrow gate; for the gate is wide and the way is broad that leads to destruction, and there are many that enter through it. For the gate is small and the way is narrow that leads to life, and there are few who find it." (Matthew 7:13-14)

Jesus taught it as truth. Right after Jesus made this statement about the narrow gate, He said to beware of the false prophets, who come to us in sheep's clothing, acting very nice and seeming to us to be very godly, but as Jesus says inwardly are ravenous wolves. Don't be fooled, study the word and see the truth God presents. He would never hide the truth from us and then hold us accountable afterward. The real message is in His word. That is where Jesus sends us for the truth.

When I was in high school I had some friends over and we received a call from one of my friend's sisters. She was very upset on the phone. She said she went to a party she never should have and was afraid and didn't know what to do. We knew of the people she was talking about who were throwing the party. They would go to parties and often destroy the house, and were always just looking to gratify themselves however they wanted at that moment. We went to the house to bring her home and when we got there the house even looked ominous from the outside. Dark and scary with sounds coming from inside that gave a clear impression it was not a place that you would want to be. A thrown beer bottle randomly thrown broke on the path as we started toward the house. Once inside we began to look for her.

What happened when we found her makes me think of Christ and what He does for us when He finds us. My friend took his wrestling team jacket, given only to the starters on the team, ones which were highly sought after, having to be relinquished if you lost a challenge match for your position. They were difficult to keep, and considered an honor to have at our school, one's people competed fiercely for. They were a sure sign of power in our little world and commanded respect. So after he took it off he wrapped it around my friend's sister, covering her. Instantly, people that were around her moved away. They instantly and unmistakably knew that she now in a sense *belonged to him*, and would have to go through him first to get to her. She was safe, saved.

THE MOST JEWISH THING I COULD DO

I love the idea of someone having to go through Jesus before they can get to me, because no one is stronger. Jesus pulls us out of evil, evil that we were all a part of, from slavery to sin, and rescues us from darkness and its control on us. He takes the punishment for our sin and we are covered by His goodness, then are protected and are brought into His family. And just like that night no one was strong enough to do anything about it. Jesus said no one can snatch them from My hand and He meant it (John 10:28-29). No one could touch one of His children.

We have to never let ourselves lose sight of the wonderful gift of salvation God secured for us as believers in Him, and how much He suffered to accomplish it, so we could be free and walk right out from the midst of evil untouched and into His loving arms. If we sat down and even tried to conceive of a greater gift, we could never do it. As I heard a well-known Bible teacher once say, "Save a man from cancer, and something else will get him. Save a man from hell, and nothing can touch him." We can never let ourselves grow accustomed to His grace, grace and mercy without which we are all lost for eternity. We can never take His holiness and what separates us from Him, namely our lack of holiness, lightly. We must hold on tightly and with tears to the access and allowance to the throne of God and His magnificent presence. He is sharing the glory of His kingdom with us who have only rebelled. We should be overwhelmed and grateful and ready to give all we have to One who did not withhold anything He had from us, but sacrificed all to redeem us. We need to think about what we hold back from God. What is it in all of our lives that we are unwilling to give up for Him?

Remember in the Bible when Jesus died it was said that the curtain in the temple which kept people out of the Holy of Holies was rent in two. It was so thick no man or group of men could have done that. The curtain is still rent in two now. It is marvelous. I thank God that I came to Christ from the Old Testament side of the cross. What a privilege we now have to boldly approach the magnificent throne of the Holy God (Hebrews 4:16). To be able to enter the Holy of Holies covered with the righteousness of Christ as our great shield.

9

The Resurrection and the Messiah

The miracles of Jesus are there as signs, signs that point to a greater reality, that of the power of God. They are displaying that power. They are displayed to confirm that the one who is doing them is indeed from God. This could be a prophet performing a miracle such as Elijah on Mt. Carmel, or the apostles healing a man lame from birth, all of these confirming the source, God Himself. God performed these miracles personally or through His spokesman to validate who they are and what they are teaching. Jesus said if you see Me casting out Satan from the finger of God (which is saying by the power of the Holy Spirit) you know the kingdom of God is upon you. With His presence on earth the kingdom of God certainly was upon us (Luke 11:20).

God had reveled Himself to Moses and proved to Moses who He was (Exodus 3:6). Just God's presence there was enough for Moses to know who He was. God then told Moses to go to Egypt and speak to the Pharaoh for Him (Exodus 3:10). Moses asked the Lord how will *they* know that he had been sent by God as God will not appear to them? God told Moses to throw his staff on the ground, and it became a snake. Then the Lord told him to reach out and grab the snake by the tail and he did it and it became a staff in his hand. He said that He did these things that they might believe that he was indeed sent by God (Exodus 4:1-5). Moses went to Egypt and performed those and many more signs and wonders to prove he was indeed sent from God.

The greatest of all signs that God ever offered was that of the resurrection of Jesus Christ.

The Resurrection verifies the claims of Christ, as did His other miracles. He claimed to be God, He claimed to be the Messiah, and proved it by predicting it and then by rising from the dead. So this is critical to Jesus' claims and to our faith as we shall see in this chapter. Beware of people who are running around today claiming to perform bona fide miracles all the time in their ministries.

So the Resurrection is that important. The Resurrection is absolutely essential to our faith.

Romans chapter ten verse nine,

> *"that if you confess with your mouth Jesus as Lord, and believe in your heart that God raised Him from the dead, you will be saved."* (Romans 10:9)

It is an essential belief of our faith. It is essential to our salvation. It shows how the sacrifice of Christ is acceptable before God. Of course He would be raised; death could never hold Him, because He is without sin. Jesus claimed to be God and He proved it through His resurrection.

Acts 17:30-31,

> *"Therefore having overlooked the times of ignorance, God is now declaring to men that all people everywhere should repent, 31-because He has fixed a day in which He will judge the world in righteousness through a man whom He has appointed, <u>having furnished proof to all men by raising Him from the dead.</u>"*

To God, the resurrection is considered sufficient proof for all men to believe the claims of God. As a consequence of that proof, they should repent, turn from their ungodly ways and ask God for forgiveness.

In the course of a conversation I was having with a woman regarding the Christian faith, she told me that she didn't believe in the resurrection. This woman had told me however that she was a Christian. Before I go into the specifics of our conversation, we have to note here what was said above. The resurrection of Christ is one of the essentials elements of the Christian faith. Essential, meaning that without it, it is no longer the Christian faith we are talking about. It is akin to saying you don't believe Jesus is God but you confess to be a Christian. Without the deity of Christ you have something different than Biblical Christianity. People are certainly free to believe whatever they wish in our country and we should uphold that. But when someone wants to take something out that is essential to defining what a particular thing is, when you do that, when you remove it, you have made it into something else. It is essential; it can't be removed without changing what you started with. If Christianity means something in particular to define it, you can't remove that and still have Christianity. The resurrection is one of those things. I will explain why that is the case.

The Bible is very clear in this. In first Corinthians chapter fifteen God's opinion on the matter is presented in an iron-clad logical fashion. We see what happens when you try to remove the reality of the resurrection from Christianity. First off in chapter fifteen the apostle Paul presents the gospel, the good news of our salvation to which the resurrection is an integral part.

He says in verse 1,

> "Now I make known to you brethren, the gospel which I preached to you, which also you received, in which also you stand."

In verse 2,

> "By which also you are saved, if you hold fast to the word which I preached to you, unless you believed in vain."
> (1Corinthians 15:1-2)

The preaching of the gospel is the tool that God chooses to use for our salvation. It carries with it the power of God (Romans 1:16). God alone has the power to change the heart, to take someone who is spiritually dead (Ephesians 2:1; Colossians 2:13), and make them alive again. The message of this good news is delivered by us through preaching as God has ordained, and the Holy Spirit removes the scales from the listener's eyes and changes the heart. The Holy Spirit regenerates them, makes them alive spiritually. That gospel message, that good news includes the resurrection of Christ as absolutely vital to believe, and how this is according to the Scriptures which are the word of God. He writes in verse three of First Corinthians chapter fifteen how this is of first importance, this message of grace, and then delivers the gospel.

This is not a tangential matter, it is of first importance, it is the gospel of our salvation. This is a story of how we are saved.

> *"For I delivered to you as <u>of first importance</u> what I also received, that Christ died for our sins according to the Scriptures. 4-and that He was buried, and that <u>He was raised on the</u> third day according to the Scriptures, 5-and that He appeared to Cephas, then to the twelve. 6-After that He appeared to more than five hundred brethren at one time, most of whom remain until now, but some have fallen asleep; 7-then He appeared to James, then to all the apostles; 8-then last of all, as to one untimely born, He appeared to me also."* (1 Corinthians 15:3-8)

So that is the good news or gospel of our faith in succinct form. Jesus died for our sins, in our place, took all of the punishments we deserved for our sins. He truly died, then He was buried, and then on the third day He rose again.

The resurrection appearances provided support, evidence for the reality of the resurrection, and we will cover that when we discuss proof for the resurrection.

The apostle then moves to answer what would be the consequences if the resurrection had not occurred at all and what that means in terms of our faith. He addressed this because some in the Corinthian church were struggling with the idea of the resurrection, saying there is no resurrection. This could have been due to influences of Greek philosophy, which is grounded in the idea of Dualism, which holds that anything physical was intrinsically evil. This made the idea of the resurrection untenable to them. They did believe the soul to be immortal. As well, there could have been an influence from the Sadducees, a sect of the Jews that did not believe in the possibility of resurrection.

He says in verse twelve,

> *"Now if Christ is preached, that He has been raised from the dead, how do some of you say that there is no resurrection?"* (1 Corinthians 15:12)

The people had heard the gospel, the true gospel. The message was simple and clear. Jesus taught about it often (John 5:28, 29; 6:44; 11:25; 14:19). This was plainly the message but some in the Corinthian community would believe in it.

In verse thirteen,

> *"But if there is no resurrection of the dead, not even Christ has been raised;"* (1 Corinthians 15:13)

Paul begins with the consequences if resurrection after death is not true. First off, Christ Himself was not raised from the dead.

Verse fourteen,

> *"And if Christ has not been raised, then our preaching is in vain, your faith also is in vain."* (1 Corinthians 15:14)

Here is where the crucial nature of the resurrection is stated. If Christ has not been resurrected as claimed, the preaching we do, the telling of the good news, reading the Bible, hearing the words of salvation read to us in church, is all for nothing, and means nothing. The faith that we have, the faith that we profess in Jesus, all of it. The faith that calls Him God and believes in the promises He made to us, and the faith we have in Christ, all are in vain. It is useless, futile and hopeless. This is what we are presented with in the word of God.

We cannot profess to be Christians and say that there is no resurrection or that it is not possible, because without it, our faith is all for naught. Our faith becomes a vacuous faith, a faith without content or substance.

In verse fifteen the inevitable conclusion goes on,

> *"Moreover, we are even found to be false witnesses of God, because we testified against God that He raised*

Christ, whom He did not raise, if in fact the dead are not raised." (1 Corinthians 15:15)

We then go from bad to worse for now we are testifying falsely about God Himself. We know from Scripture the serious nature of preaching something falsely about God as in the Book of Galatians, and in this situation if the resurrection has indeed not occurred, we become false witnesses against Him. We are lying to the world. One of the Ten Commandments, the top ten Laws according to God is not to bear false witness. This goes back to what was said before in this book about embracing other religions or views about Christ, and that we should accept all views as true in the name of tolerance. Here we see that if we preach falsely that we are testifying falsely against God, and we can see here in this passage that this is not something we are supposed to do and is presented as a serious matter.

Verses sixteen through seventeen,

> *For if the dead are not raised, not even Christ has been raised; and if Christ has not been raised, your faith is worthless; you are still in your sins.* (1Corinthians 15:17)

If there is no resurrection then no one is saved, there is no redemption, for anyone. Jesus then is not God as He claimed, He is not in heaven. If He cannot redeem Himself, He certainly cannot redeem us, so then it would make no sense to believe that He could.

In verse eighteen,

> *Then those who have fallen asleep in Christ have perished.* (1 Corinthians 15:18)

This would mean that all of the believers who have ever lived and have since died are still dead and that is it.

In verse nineteen,

> *If we have hoped in Christ in this life only, we are of all men the most to be pitied.* (1 Corinthians 15:19)

When we go out to preach the gospel in the world, we encounter many different reactions, some are happy, some are indifferent, some insulted. If indeed there is no resurrection, when we go out to tell people of the gospel of the Christian faith, people should show no other reaction to us other than pity. Even to people who are vehemently opposed to the message, and I have met some like this in conversations before, they should not be angry with us, or should even argue strenuously against it getting extremely upset, they shouldn't feel anger or even hatred, they should feel sorry for us. If there is no resurrection, we are then the most to be pitied. It is important that we realize why the Bible tells us this. It is not only because we believe in our faith for nothing, that when we die nothing happens to us, and we just decompose. That's of course the biggest reason, but there's more.

We are told this because of the sacrifice involved in the Christian life. This is reminiscent of false teachers who promise us wealth and prosperity when we embrace Jesus. They promise that our lives will be easy, that you should have and could have all you ask for, all you dream of. The reality is Christ tells us we will have tribulation. He said that they hated Him and that they will hate us if we represent Him in the world. He also said that we will share in His humiliation as well as His glory, and that if we don't share in His humiliation we are not worthy of His kingdom.

We are to be pitied because a Christian life involves sacrifice for Christ, denying ourselves and picking up our cross, and being persecuted because of what we believe. As I have mentioned previously, this is not talked about much today but our Lord talked very much about it. We follow His teaching, and His example. If someone tells us something contrary to that we don't follow that advice. We have great joy, but this is in the midst of suffering in this life. We know the future that awaits us, and then end of tribulation with it, eternity in heaven. This is our hope, this is our joy (2 Tim. 3:12, 1 Pet. 4:12-19, Matt. 5:10).

The apostle spells this out in relation to his own life and the trials he endured, in verses thirty through thirty two, of the futility of living a Christian life if there is no resurrection.

> *"Why are we also in danger every hour?*
> *I affirm, brethren, by the boasting in you which I have*
> *in Christ Jesus our Lord, I die daily.*

> *If from human motives I fought with wild beats at Ephesus, what does it profit me? If the dead are not raised,* LET US EAT AND DRINK, FOR TOMORROW WE DIE." (1 Corinthians 15:30-32)

If there is no resurrection there is no reason to undergo the persecution of being a Christian, of living in opposition to the ways of the world, of giving up the pleasures that men naturally seek to fulfill. If there is nothing but this life we should "Go for the gusto," as beer commercials tell us. We would indeed be fools to live self sacrificing lives for Christ and for others if this is true.

In discussing the resurrection and the skepticism that many hold to today in regards to its reality it is necessary to see that when people take such a position they are opposing what Christ Himself spoke on the matter. We had mentioned previously about a sect of the Jews called the Sadducees who did not believe that any resurrection is possible for anyone. It is interesting to note that Jesus had a debate with them, in which the Sadducees tried to ask Him a question regarding the resurrection and life in heaven, to confound Jesus and discredit Him as a teacher (Matthew 22:23-33).

Jesus answered them by saying that they were mistaken, not understanding the Scriptures or the power of God. He stated the reality of the resurrection in the discussion, and how God was not the God of the dead but of the living, that clearly these people He is about to mention were still alive, by saying *"I am the God of Abraham, Isaac, and of Jacob, He is not the God of the dead but of the living"* (Matthew 22:32), ending the whole debate on the authority of the Scriptures with the tense of a verb (I am the God, not I was). This is important today because many people don't hold the Scriptures in high regard or as the Word of God which it claims. Jesus called the Scriptures God speaking to us, in verse thirty one of Matthew twenty two, and argues from Scriptures with the slightest detail of it (in this case verb tense), having major importance.

It is also used by Jesus as the final arbiter (See His confrontation with Satan in Matthew 4:1-11, and what Jesus used in each case to fight the devil and end each discussion).

Also Jesus predicted His own resurrection before it occurred, certainly teaching of its reality. If people want to go contrary to anything Jesus clearly believed such as His resurrection, they are in a precarious position to say the least. For He did present Himself as the Creator of all things, the Almighty God. As well He is referred to as the Chief Cornerstone, the Stone that the builders rejected as prophesied in the Old Testament in Daniel 2:44-45; Psalm 118:22,23; Isaiah 28:16, and referred to in the New Testament in Romans 9:33; 1 Peter 2:6-9; Luke 20:18. This is a prophecy of the coming Messiah, the Christ, the Anointed One. Jesus points this out to the Jewish leaders who rejected Him and warned them. They clearly knew what He was talking about and their reaction is evident of that.

He said in Luke chapter 20:17-18, But Jesus looked at them and said, *"What then is this that is written:*
'THE STONE WHICH THE BUILDERS REJECTED, THIS BECAME THE CHIEF CORNER STONE'?
Everyone who falls on that stone will be broken to pieces; but on whomever it falls, it will scatter him like dust." (Luke 20:17-18)

To be in an opposing position of Jesus is not a favorable place to be. There is nothing above Him, those who reject Him have no hope (Ephesians 2:12). He is our hope, graciously given to us because He is a merciful God. Verse 14 of Ephesians 2 says that He is our peace (Ephesians 2:14). We have peace with God through Him (Romans 5:1).

So we have the testimony of the Bible to the authenticity of the resurrection. Jesus clearly held to this view and we have that testimony in the Scriptures for us today. There are also other proofs of an historical nature for the reliability of the resurrection account.

To start with the Christian faith grew up in the very same area where all of the miracles of the faith occurred. It is highly unlikely for a hoax to be perpetrated there where people could easily refute it. They live there and could walk up when they were preaching and ask, "What in the world are you talking about, we live here and no one ever heard of any of that happening here?" That is not what occurred. The Christian faith grew quickly right in the same region where the miracles were purported to occur.

Paul's account of the resurrection was written very soon after it occurred. Lee Strobel reports in his book, The Case for Christ,

"We know that Paul wrote 1 Corinthians between A.D. 55 and 57. He indicates in First Corinthians fifteen one through four that he has already passed on this creed to the church at Corinth, which would mean it must predate his visit there in A.D. 51. Therefore the creed was being used within twenty years of the resurrection, which is quite early.

"However, I'd agree with the various scholars who trace it back even further, to within two to eight years of the resurrection, or from about A.D. 32 to 38, when Paul received it in either Damascus or Jerusalem. So this is incredibly early material-primitive, unadorned testimony to the fact that Jesus appeared alive to skeptics like Paul and James, as well as to Peter and the rest of the disciples."[16]

So in 1 Corinthians 15 the presentation of the gospel, there is part of a very early creed that started soon after the resurrection of Christ. Paul states the gospel and then evidences for it. He lists the appearances of Jesus to his disciples including appearing to 500 at one time. He adds some of whom are dead but many of whom remain until now. He is saying most of them are alive, essentially the point is, "Many are still alive, go ask them."

This also prevents people from saying that the resurrection story was the result of myth or legend. Historians who study this area of history, the rate of development of myth or legend agree in this case. There was no where near enough time for the development of myth or legend to have occurred.

Muller's critique is still valid today and is confirmed by A.N. Sherwin-White, a historian of Greek and Roman times. Professor Sherwin-White is not a theologian; he is a professional historian of the times prior and contemporaneous with Jesus. According to Sherwin-White, the sources for Greek and Roman history are usually biased and removed one or two generations or even centuries from the events they

---

[16] The Case for Christ, Lee Strobel, pg. 230

record. Yet, he says, historians reconstruct with confidence the course of Roman and Greek history.

When Sherwin-White turns to the gospels, he states that for the gospels to be legends, the rate of legendary accumulation would have to be "unbelievable." More generations would be needed.

The writings of Herodotus enable us to determine the rate at which legend accumulates, and the tests show that even two generations is too short a time span to allow legendary tendencies to wipe out the hard core of historical facts.

Julius Muller challenged scholars of the mid-nineteenth century to show anywhere in history where within thirty years of a great series of legends had accumulated around a historical individual and had become firmly fixed in general belief. Muller's challenge has never been met.

It is also important to note how professor Sherwin-White talks of the great gap between the sources that historians have for many ancient works, and the sources we have for the Bible. If we look at most of the time gaps in history of the earliest sources of writings that historians have and the original time of the occurrence of the events it is startling. Yet historians have no problem with these time gaps when presenting this information gleaned from these historians to their students in history class.

> "The two earliest biographies of Alexander the Great were written by Arian and Plutarch more than four hundred years after Alexander's death in 323 B.C., yet historians believe them to be generally trustworthy."[17]

We have thousands of Greek manuscripts of the New Testament available today which were written within the lifetimes of the writers.

In addition, the accounts of the resurrection lack fantastic, unrealistic, magical elements characteristic of myths and fables. It was reported very soberly and without the bizarre characteristics of myth. The story is told in a very direct fashion and with some very unlikely descriptions if it was indeed invented or conjured up.

---

[17] The Case for Christ, Lee Strobel, pg. 33

First off, the discoverers of the empty tomb were women. This is incredible in light of the value of testimony of women in the ancient world. Their testimony would be considered worthless in a court of Law. At that time women were very much second-class citizens with very few rights. There are ancient Rabbinic writings that state, that it would be better if the Law of God be burnt than to be given to a woman. As well, they write that blessed is the man who child is male, and cursed is the man who child is female. So the fact the writers of the New Testament report women as discovering the body of Jesus is incredible and lends credence to their testimony.

In addition, the disciples report that they were in hiding with the door locked when the women came to them to tell them of the risen Christ. This admission, again especially with the role of women in society at the time adds further credence.

The resurrection accounts also have Joseph of Arimathea as requesting the body of Jesus from Pontius Pilate for burial. This man was a member of the Jewish Sanhedrin, of which the other members, not Joseph, plotted and then had Jesus executed.

They were clearly enemies of the Christian faith and continued to be into the accounts of the disciples and their persecution of them in the book of Acts. Again it is highly unlikely to have an enemy of the faith be a hero in the story.

No one disputed the empty tomb. The earliest argument that the Jewish leaders proposed against the resurrection of Jesus was that the disciples stole the body. This argument presupposes the empty tomb.

If this was not true it would have been so easy for enemies of the faith to stop the spread of this faith by taking the body out of the tomb and parading it around the streets of Jerusalem. In addition, the writings of the Rabbis in the period after Jesus' death, do not deny the miracles of Jesus, to which of course the resurrection is one, but rather they say He performed the miracles by the power of the devil.

As well, the tomb was guarded and by Roman guards, who were part of the most sophisticated, and well-trained army in the world, and who would be killed if one of their prisoners escaped. They were instructed to guard this body for that very reason, so the body would not disappear as Jesus predicted. The disciples were in hiding as we have said and certainly not in any position for a daring theft attempt. If for some outrageous reason they could have stolen the body, which we see is preposterous, they would have suffered and endured dreadful persecution all for a hoax they perpetrated. All of Jesus' apostles went to a martyr's death with the exception of the apostle John. They were continually tortured as well throughout their lives. Would they suffer all this for a lie? People may be willing to die for something they believed to be the true as we see with terrorists today. But such men as these believe that they are doing this for God and will be rewarded in paradise.

The disciples went from "fearful," hiding behind locked doors (before the resurrection) to "fearless" (after witnessing the resurrection), powerful undaunted preachers of the truth of Christ. Peter, in a complete transformation of character, stood before the Jewish Sanhedrin and accused them of killing Jesus and warned them of the judgment involved as the Book of Acts describes (Acts 4:10). He was told not to speak of these things again and was beaten for that, but despite the extreme pain, and nothing as we would have now with our modern medicines to relieve it, openly and loudly praised God and rejoiced to suffer for His name. Being flogged in those days was no small matter as we will see.

Imagine testing the pain of flogging today by removing your shirt and having someone hit you, even once, as hard as they could with a whip, can you imagine the pain? Think of how many times the apostle Paul was beaten for preaching the gospel and continued. A modern missionary reported his experiences while being held in prison in a foreign country for preaching the gospel. On one occasion they tortured him by beating him across his back with rods. He said it felt like his back was in fire, he couldn't believe the pain. He said he doesn't know how the apostle Paul endured being tortured so many times. All this, for a lie, I think not.

Medical expert, Alexander Metherell, M.D., shed light on the subject on Roman floggings. "The Roman floggings were known to be terribly brutal. They usually consisted of thirty-nine lashes but frequently were a lot more than that, depending on the mood of the soldier applying the blows. The soldier would use a whip of braided leather thongs with metal balls woven into them. When the whip would strike the flesh, these balls would cause deep bruises or contusions, which would break open with further blows. And the whip had pieces of sharp bone as well, which would cut the flesh severely. The back would be so shredded that part of the spine was sometimes exposed by the deep, deep cuts. The whipping would have gone all the way from the shoulders down to the back, the buttocks, and the back of the legs. It was just terrible."[18]

He goes on, One physician who has studied Roman beatings said, 'As the flogging continued, the lacerations would tear the underlying skeletal muscles produce quivering ribbons of bleeding flesh.' A third-century historian by the name of Eusebius described a flogging by saying, 'The sufferer's veins were laid bare, and the very muscles, sinews, and the bowels of the victim were open to exposure.'"[19]

This is relevant to our next discussion which discusses some alternate theories that have arisen in the past to explain away the resurrection. We have to remember that all this beating that was described above occurred before Jesus even went to the cross. Most of these alternate theories have fallen out of favor due to the amount of evidence to the contrary, and are not seriously considered anymore.

One of those is the Swoon Theory. This suggests that Jesus did not really die on the cross and then revived in the cool, dark tomb, and walked out. This is implausible for several reasons. First off, as we mentioned earlier when discussing the guards at the tomb, if a Roman soldier lost his prisoner, or if he survived, the soldier would be killed. The flogging alone that the Romans inflicted to the prisoners set for crucifixion could kill you. If you survived, you would be in no shape to get out of a tomb, get past the guards and walk anywhere, let alone motivate people to follow you in that shape. Crucifixion was gruesome to say the least. Huge spikes were driven through your wrists and ankles. You hung there until you died unable to hold yourself up and you suffocate, and the Roman soldiers made sure of that, again as they were responsible.

One of the ways they would speed the death of the prisoner was to

---

[18] The Case for Christ, Lee Strobel, pg. 195
[19] abid., pg. 195

break his legs, that way he could not try to lift himself up while on the cross, allowing him to breathe.

John records the events at the end of Jesus' life in chapter 19 of his gospel. In verse 32,

> *So the soldiers came, and broke the legs of the first man and the other who was crucified with Him; 33-but coming to Jesus, when they saw that He was already dead, they did not break His legs. 34-But one of the soldiers pierced His side with a spear, and immediately blood and water came out.* (John 19:32)

John's description lends credence to his testimony. This is attested to again by medical expert Alexander Metherell, M.D;

> "Even before He died -and this is important too-the hypovolemic shock would have caused a sustained rapid heart rate that would have contributed to heart failure, resulting n the collection of fluid in the membrane around the heart, called a pericardial effusion, as well as around the lungs, which is called a pleural effusion."
>
> "Why is that significant?"
>
> "Because of what happened when the Roman soldier came around and, being fairly certain that Jesus was dead, confirmed it by thrusting a spear into His right side; that's not certain, but from the description it was probably the right side, between the ribs.
>
> "The spear apparently went through the right lung and into the heart, so when the spear was pulled out, some fluid-the pericardial effusion and the pleural effusion-came out. This would have had the appearance of a clear fluid, like water, followed by a large volume of blood, as the eyewitness John described in his gospel."[20]

---

[20] The Case for Christ, Lee Strobel, pg. 199

The greatest testimony however we could have is the relationship we experience with the living Christ. We have the Holy Spirit inside us so we know that we are saved, and that what we believe is real and true (1 John 2:20,27; 4:13).

Let us join with the apostle Peter in praising God for this greatest of gifts, for the great and certain hope we have as Christians, for our future of our resurrection into heaven, into glory.

> *"Blessed be the God and Father of our Lord Jesus Christ, who according to His great mercy has caused us to be born again to a living hope through the resurrection of Jesus Christ from the dead."* (1 Peter 1:3)

www.ingramcontent.com/pod-product-compliance
Lightning Source LLC
Chambersburg PA
CBHW020004050426
42450CB00005B/300